THE GERMAN TANK DESTRUCTION BADGE

in World War II

Rolf Michaelis

Schiffer Military History
Atglen, PA

Contents

Book Translation by Dr. Edward Force.

Book Design by Stephanie Daugherty.

Library of Congress Control Number: 2011946075

Printed in China.
ISBN: 978-0-7643-4052-9

This book was originally published in German under the title
Das Sonderabzeichen für das Niederkämpfen von Panzerkampfwagen durch Einzelkämpfer.

We are interested in hearing from authors with book ideas on related topics.

Published by Schiffer Publishing Ltd.
4880 Lower Valley Road
Atglen, PA 19310
Phone: (610) 593-1777
FAX: (610) 593-2002
E-mail: Info@schifferbooks.com.
Visit our web site at: www.schifferbooks.com
Please write for a free catalog.
This book may be purchased from the publisher.
Try your bookstore first.

In Europe, Schiffer books are distributed by:
Bushwood Books
6 Marksbury Avenue
Kew Gardens
Surrey TW9 4JF, England
Phone: 44 (0) 20 8392-8585
FAX: 44 (0) 20 8392-9876
E-mail: Info@bushwoodbooks.co.uk.
Visit our website at: www.bushwoodbooks.co.uk

Foreword

The technical advances made during the Second World War were enormous and resulted in unbelievable advances in vital fields in a short time. Consider that the first operational jet fighter aircraft, the Me 262, was developed while the Hs 123 biplane was still in service.

After it had become apparent that armored vehicles were just as important as the air force, from 1941 work began on increasingly heavy tanks. These were constantly up-gunned and their armor protection was increased. A comparison is impressive: while the German Panzer IV (Sd.Kfz.161) weighed 25 tons, the Panzer VI "Tiger II" (Sd.Kfz.182) was almost three times as heavy at 70 tons!

The close-range engagement of tanks became extremely important mainly because of the Soviet T-34 and KV-I tanks, which for a long time were superior to all German tanks and anti-tank guns. The Soviets also enjoyed quantitative superiority, and the only reason that this did not lead to the collapse of the German armed forces in 1941 was the Red Army's incorrect use of tanks. Frequently employed in small groups of three to five tanks to support the infantry, they could often be put out of action with close-range weapons.

On 9 March 1942 Hitler acknowledged this style of anti-tank warfare by creating the "Special Badge for the Singlehanded Destruction of Tanks Etc.".

The purpose of this book is to provide a general account of this decoration and the close-range combating of tanks. In addition to a description of the special badge and the most commonly-used weapons, it includes operational accounts by recipients of the badge.

I would like to express my gratitude to all those who helped in the creation of this book, especially Frau Emmerich-Chrzonszcz and Herr Möckl as well as Herr Tammiksaar for the exhibits in his museum on the history of the Estonian SS Legion.

Rolf Michaelis
Berlin, March 2010

Close-Range Anti-Tank Warfare

In contrast to the brief campaigns in Poland in 1939 and Western Europe in 1940, from 1941 in the Soviet Union the Wehrmacht found itself confronted by extremes for which it was not prepared. In addition to autumn and winter weather conditions that were extremely severe by western-European standards, the Red Army proved to be quantitatively, and in some respects technically, superior to the German forces.

The German successes in 1941-42 were largely due to errors in strategy by Soviet commanders. These included the operational tactics employed by Soviet armored formations, whose T-34 and KV I tanks were superior to all German tanks and largely invulnerable to German anti-tank guns. Usually employed in penny packets without radio communications, these tanks were often put out of action by German soldiers employing close-range weapons. The 75-mm Pak 40 anti-tank gun began reaching the Eastern Front in large numbers in the second half of 1942, however there were never enough to make good the shortcomings in the German anti-tank defenses. In his study of the fighting in West Prussia in 1945, former Oberstleutnant Hans Jürgen Pantenius wrote:[1]

"Apart from the enemy's massed artillery fire at the beginning of his breakthrough offensives, the infantry's deadliest foes were the enemy's close-support aircraft and, in particular, his armored units, as the infantry divisions had little with which to oppose them: a light flak company for anti-aircraft defense and for anti-tank defense a company of towed 75-mm heavy anti-tank guns and a company of assault guns (old divisions) or a company of Hetzer tank destroyers armed with a 75-mm cannon (Volksgrenadier divisions). For reasons already put forward[2], the Panzerschreck anti-tank rocket launcher has not been a success with the regiments. For the infantry, the anti-tank defense problem has not been solved satisfactorily during the entire war."

In the beginning, when the Soviets employed their tanks in "penny packets", courageous soldiers were able to destroy them at close range, however the change in the enemy's offensive tactics in 1943 frequently led to the collapse of entire sectors of the German front. The inferior German anti-tank defense was thus an important factor in the defeat on the Eastern Front.

Conscious of these facts, the German command began emphasizing the destruction of enemy tanks at close range by individual soldiers, who were then dubbed

---

1 Pantenius, Hans Jürgen: Letzte Schlacht an der Ostfront, Hamburg 2002

2 These are contained in the chapter "Anti-Tank Weapons and Devices".

"Einzelkämpfer" or lone fighters. Pamphlet 77/3, which was conceived solely for this topic, depicted the possible methods of destroying an enemy tank from close range in a way that downplayed the dangers. In fact, thousands of German soldiers lost their lives in direct confrontations with enemy armored vehicles. Close-range assaults against enemy tanks involved the use of hand grenades, hollow charge magnetic mines, anti-tank mines, Blendkörper (literally "blinding devices", i.e. smoke grenades, etc.) and panzerfausts. While the latter at least could be fired from a certain distance, the others had to be employed in immediate proximity to the tank. As a result, the attackers were exposed to fire from escorting infantry and the tank crew.

On the other hand, close-range anti-tank weapons did offer an effective means of disabling enemy tanks. German soldiers were not alone in this respect, however. The western allies made very effective use of rocket anti-tank weapons (such as the American bazooka). These weapons took a heavy toll of German armored vehicles, especially during the offensive in the Ardennes.

The "Overcoming of Enemy Armored Vehicles" did not necessarily mean the total destruction of the tank, however. If recovered, many tanks knocked out in this way were quickly repaired and returned to service. The principal result, therefore, was to put the enemy tank out of service for a short time. The numbers reflect this. On 20 January 1945 the Wehrmacht High Command reported that 1,404 Soviet tanks had been knocked out during the fighting in the Stuhlweissenburg area and north of the Danube in Hungary during the period from 20 December 1944 to 15 January 1945. On 15 February 1945, Army Group Vistula reported that more than 1,253 tanks had been destroyed in its area during the four weeks from 14 January to 14 February 1945. The Wehrmacht daily reports frequently announced the destruction of about 200 tanks on the Eastern and Western Fronts. Of course these figures include those enemy tanks knocked out by German tanks and anti-tank guns as well as by close-range weapons. Without repairing the tanks thus damaged, the Allies would have been unable to continue their advance.

The supplements to the Wehrmacht communiqués frequently identified by name soldiers who had performed outstanding feats on the previous day. Among them were men who had singlehandedly knocked out enemy tanks. In addition to honoring these men, these reports were intended to focus attention on the importance of this mission and of course encourage their emulation:

"3 February 1945

> During the fierce fighting in Königsberg's outer defensive ring, Ernst Tilbursy, a battery commander in the Volkssturm, destroyed five Soviet tanks with the panzerfaust."

17 February 1945

> During the night of 8-9 February in the combat zone around Liegnitz, Obergefreite Walter Süß-Meyer, 10th Battery of Flak Regiment 46 (mot.), singlehandedly destroyed five enemy tanks with the panzerfaust.

23 February 1945

> During the fighting for Lauban a company of Grenadier Replacement and Training Battalion 318 under the command of Leutnant Gielnig displayed extraordinary steadfastness. In two days it destroyed eight tanks with close-range weapons. Despite an arm prosthesis, the company commander singlehandedly knocked out four Soviet tanks with the panzerfaust."

In addition to being decorated with the Special Badge, soldiers were frequently awarded the Iron Cross, Second or First Class at the same time and, when warranted, were given a 14-day special leave. Furthermore, on 7 March 1945 Hitler decreed "that every soldier who destroys six enemy tanks with the panzerfaust or makeshift weapons" could receive "the Knight's Cross of the Iron Cross". Successes with the rocket anti-tank weapon ("Stovepipe" or "Tank Terror") received special attention. Units were directed to inform the soldiers about this decree as quickly as possible, an indication of the importance attached to the destruction of enemy tanks by individual soldiers in the closing months of the war. Unlike the creation of the Special Badge for the Singlehanded Destruction of Tanks, however, the decree was not retroactive.

The original idea of using a simple and cheap weapon to destroy a much more expensive one was not realized. More than ten million panzerfausts alone were manufactured at a cost of just under 400 million Reichsmark. If one assumes that a T-34, for example, was worth about 80,000 Reichsmark, the destruction of about 20,000 Allied tanks by close-range weapons would have caused theoretical damage to the enemy economy roughly equivalent to 1.6 billion Reichsmark. As at least 50% of these tanks were surely repaired, the figure is reduced to 800 million Reichsmark. If one adds the additional cost of hollow charge magnetic mines, anti-tank mines, etc. to the German total, it becomes apparent that, from an economic point of view, the program should be viewed as no better than a marginal success.

Generalkommando XXXXVI. Pz.Korps
Abt.IIa/Ic K.Gef.Std., den 25.7.41.

Korps-Tagesbefehl.

Bei den schweren Abwehrkämpfen um Jelnja vom 23. - 25.7. wurden von SS-Div. "Reich" 5[illegible] Feindpanzer abgeschossen, darunter 8 schwere Panzer (T 28).

Hierbei zeichneten sich besonders aus:

1.) SS-Untersturmführer W e i s e n b a c h und
SS-Unterscharführer E h m,
welche auf die schweren Pz.Kampfwagen sprangen, die Besatzung durch Pistolenschüsse durch die Sehschlitze bekämpften und die Panzer durch Sprengladungen und Uebergiessen mit Brennstoff in Brand setzten, nachdem die Panzerkampfwagen weder durch Pak (3,7 cm) noch durch s. J.G. ausser Gefecht gesetzt werden konnten.

2.) SS-Unterscharführer S t e n g e r, 11./SS-"Deutschland," welcher am 25.7. mit 2 M.G.'s den Angriff von 1½ Btl. roter Jnfanterie längere Zeit bis
Die 11./SS-"Deutschland" unte
K u m p f machte aus eigen
zu blutigen Verlusten des Ge
Hierbei wurden 3 Panzer, 5
6 s.M.G., 5 l.M.G. und eine

Jch spreche für diese vo
meine vollste Anerkennung aus.

The action described above is typical of the close-combat tactics employed against Soviet tanks early in the Eastern Campaign.

Among the decorations worn by SS-Unterscharführer Ehm (German Cross in Gold on 16/9/43) is the unofficial version Tank Destruction Badge for the destruction of five tanks, consisting of a golden tank on silver band.

A pioneer of the SS-Totenkopf Division. In addition to the Iron Crosses, First and Second Class, the General Assault Badge and the Wound Badge in Black, he wears two Tank Destruction Badges.

An explosion blew the turret off the hull of this Soviet tank.

In 1944/45 it was not uncommon for as many as 200 enemy tanks to be destroyed in one day. This resulted in an impressive monthly figure of up to 6,000 tanks. Below is a report by Army Group Vistula dated 15 February 1945.

Winter 1944/45.

The Tank Destruction Badge

After the shortcomings in German anti-tank weapons made the close-range engagement of tanks an important pillar of the eastern campaign of 1941, on 9 March 1942 Hitler approved a proposal by the Army High Command to introduce a special decoration:

"1. The Führer authorizes the introduction of a special badge for the destruction of tanks by individual soldiers.

2. The special badge is to be awarded to soldiers who, on or after 22 June 1941, have singlehandedly destroyed or put out of action an enemy tank or other enemy armored vehicle in close combat using close-range weapons or close-range devices (anti-tank rifle, rifle grenade, hand grenade cluster, etc.).

3. The badge consists of a band of spun aluminum fabric approximately 90 mm long and 32 mm wide with two woven black stripes (3 mm wide), on which is mounted the stamped metal silhouette of a tank.

4. If awarded again, an additional arm band will be put on."

On 23 October 1941, even before the special badge was created, the Army High Command had taken steps to ensure that this act of bravery was properly acknowledged, decreeing that personal actions resulting in the destruction of an enemy tank would be considered an assault attack as per the requirements for the awarding of the Assault Badge. In addition to general acknowledgement in the form of the Iron Cross, Second or First Class, each tank knocked out was counted as an assault day (Sturmtag) toward the earning of an assault badge (Infantry Assault Badge, General Assault Badge, Tank Battle Badge or later the Ground Battle Badge). Consequently the awarding of the appropriate assault badge followed automatically after the destruction of three tanks.

After the introduction of the new decoration, a small batch of badges was sent to each unit. On 30 June 1942 the SS Police Division noted in its report on the awarding of orders and decorations that the division had initially been sent nine badges, of which three had been awarded to members of the division retroactive to 22 June 1941.

After a number of soldiers had repeatedly taken out enemy tanks and thus wore a number of special badges, on 18 December 1943 the Army High Command announced the introduction of another badge:

> "The Special Badge on Golden Band will be awarded after the fifth certifiable destruction of tanks etc. in place of another silver special badge. The four silver badges previously awarded will be taken down and retained as keepsakes by the soldier in question."

The official version of a black tank on a golden band was supplemented by unofficial models consisting of golden tanks on silver bands or golden tanks on gold bands, which were worn by recipients. Oberleutnant Günther Viezenz (10th Company/Grenadier Regiment 7) was an especially successful "tank cracker". He knocked out a total of 21 vehicles and ultimately wore four gold versions of the badge and one silver.

The badges were awarded by the battalion commander at the suggestion of the unit commander (usually the company commander). The enemy tank or armored vehicle had to have been put out of action through the personal actions of the soldier, using the anti-tank weapons described in the following text. Initially, those weapons that could be used from a distance were not considered for the awarding of the Special Badge, as their use was not regarded as close combat in the true sense of the word. Not until the order of 18 December 1943 were they. too, officially recognized as meeting the requirements for the awarding of the Special Badge.

In contrast to the other military orders and decorations of the Third Reich, no award certificate was supposed to accompany the Special Badge for the Single-handed Destruction of Tanks. Instead, the soldiers were only given a certified copy of the battalion order. In fact, however, various units (possibly through misunderstanding of the order) produced a variety of award certificates on their own initiative. These ranged from simple mimeographed award certificates to documents resembling decorative pages.

The awarding of the Special Badge was entered in the soldier's personal papers (pay book, Wehrpass (military service book) and Wehrstammbuch (military record book)). Each soldier was presented just one badge, which was to be sewn on the upper right sleeve of the field blouse. Subsequent badges could be procured from decorations stores in the homeland on presentation of the pay book or certified battalion order.

The Special Badge could also be awarded posthumously if the soldier was killed during the successful engagement of an enemy tank. In this case the certified battalion order was to be sent to the bereaved with the badge as a keepsake.

The Special Badge consisted of a band (approx. 90 x 32 mm) of spun aluminum thread with two 3-mm-wide woven black stripes, on which was mounted a stamped metal silhouette of a tank (approx. 44 x 18 mm) in black. Astonishingly, the short-barreled version of the German Panzer IV served as the model and not the well-known Soviet T-34. There was a counter-plate (approx. 54 x 21 mm) on the reverse, through which the three short metal tabs on the tank were bent, thus fixing it to the band. The tank and counter-plate were made of sheet iron or refined zinc. A patch of green, blue or black uniform fabric was glued over the counter-plate.

As a rule, the so-called "Tank Destruction Badge" was delivered by the various manufacturers in small cellophane or paper bags. The bands and tanks produced by the various manufacturers displayed certain differences. Some tanks appeared rather small, others bulky. The bands displayed certain variations in color, not all of which can be attributed to being stored for the past 65 years.

Altogether, just under 20,000 Special Badges were awarded, including about 400 examples with the golden band.

Wearing five (!)Tank Destruction Badges, Adolf Peichl (on the left) congratulates a comrade on his success against an enemy tank. Peichl himself destroyed 11 tanks and on 26 October 1943 was awarded the Golden Close Combat Bar. Wounded a number of times, he also wears the Wound Badge in Gold. Peichl was awarded the Knight's Cross of the Iron Cross on 16/10/1944.

Publication of the Tank Destruction Badge.

Anlage 4.

Auszeichnungen.

Sonderabzeichen für das Niederkämpfen von Panzerkampfwagen mit Nahkampfmitteln.

Der Führer hat die Einführung eines Sonderabzeichens für das Niederkämpfen von Panzerkampfwagen durch Einzelkämpfer genehmigt.

Das Sonderabzeichen wird an Soldaten verliehen, die ab 22. Juni 1941 als Einzelkämpfer mit Nahkampfwaffen oder Nahkampfmitteln (Panzerbüchse, Gewehrgranate, geballte Ladung usw.) einen feindlichen Panzerkampfwagen oder ein sonstiges feindliches gepanzertes Fahrzeug im Nahkampf vernichtet oder außer Gefecht gesetzt haben.

Für jeden vernichteten Panzerkampfwagen wird je ein Sonderabzeichen verliehen.

Das Sonderabzeichen wird am rechten Oberärmel der Feldbluse getragen (H.V.Bl. 1942, Teil B, Ziffer 190).

Sturmabzeichen.

Die Vernichtung von Panzerkampfwagen im Nahkampf gilt außerdem als Sturmangriff.

Der persönliche Einsatz bei der Erledigung feindlicher Panzerkampfwagen im Nahkampf mit Nahkampfwaffen oder Nahkampfmitteln gilt als Sturmangriff im Sinne der Bestimmungen über die Verleihung der Sturmabzeichen (H.V.Bl. 1941, Teil C, Ziff. 907).

An Obergefreiter of the Panzer Grenadier Division "Grossdeutschland" is presented the Tank Destruction Badge.

From top to bottom:

Two Special Badges on silver band. The production differences are obvious.

Below: three badges, each representing the destruction of five tanks.

First the official version with a black tank on a golden band.

And two unofficial versions, a golden tank on a golden band and a golden tank on a silver band.

Numerous companies produced the badges, and dimensions, especially of the metal parts, varied.

The Tank Destruction Badge broken down into its components.

Dimensions: approx. 90 x 32 mm.

Reverse side cover made of uniform fabric.

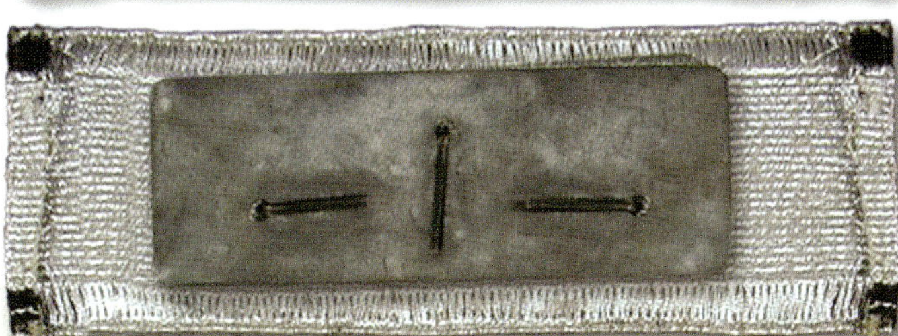

The metal tank was attached to the woven aluminum fabric by three blunt folding tabs.

Dimensions of the backing plate approx. 55 x 20 mm.

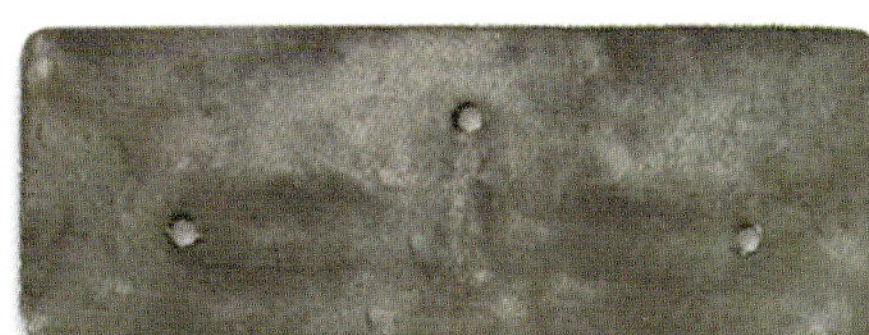

Dimensions of the tank approx. 43 x 18 mm.

Combating tanks from close range was not quite as amusing as depicted in the photo on the left.

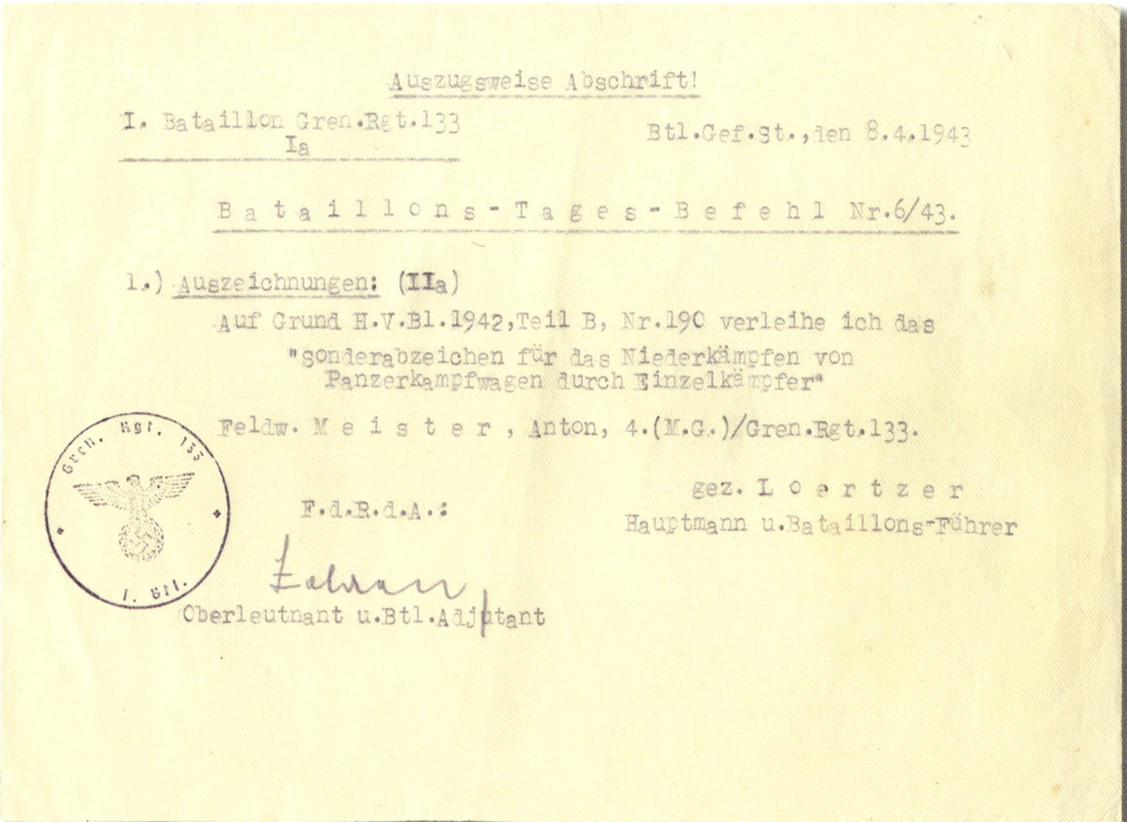

Auszugsweise Abschrift!

I. Bataillon Gren.Rgt.133
Ia

Btl.Gef.St., den 8.4.1943

Bataillons-Tages-Befehl Nr.6/43.

1.) Auszeichnungen: (IIa)

Auf Grund H.V.Bl.1942, Teil B, Nr.190 verleihe ich das "Sonderabzeichen für das Niederkämpfen von Panzerkampfwagen durch Einzelkämpfer"

Feldw. Meister, Anton, 4.(M.G.)/Gren.Rgt.133.

gez. Loertzer
Hauptmann u.Bataillons-Führer

F.d.R.d.A.:

Oberleutnant u.Btl.Adjutant

Gren. Rgt. 133
I. Btl.

Interestingly, soldiers awarded the Tank Destruction Badge were only given a copy of the battalion order instead of an award certificate. Like all decorations, however, the Special Badge was entered in the soldier's personal papers.

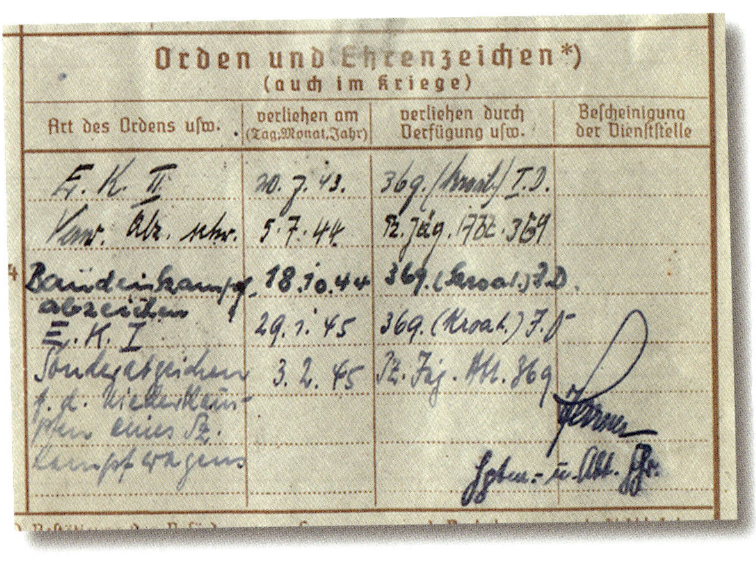

Orden und Ehrenzeichen*)
(auch im Kriege)

Art des Ordens usw.	verliehen am (Tag, Monat, Jahr)	verliehen durch Verfügung usw.	Bescheinigung der Dienststelle
E.K. II	20.7.43.	369.(Kroat.) I.D.	
Verw. Abz. schw.	5.7.44	Pz.Jäg. Abt. 369	
Bandenkampfabzeichen	18.10.44	369.(Kroat.) I.D.	
E.K. I	29.1.45	369.(Kroat.) I.D.	
Sonderabzeichen f. d. Niederkämpfen eines Pz. Kampfwagens	3.2.45	Pz.Jg. Abt. 369	[illegible]

Recorded on this page from a Wehrpass are the Iron Cross, Second Class, the Wound Badge in Black, the Anti-Partisan War Badge, the Iron Cross, First Class and a Tank Destruction Badge.

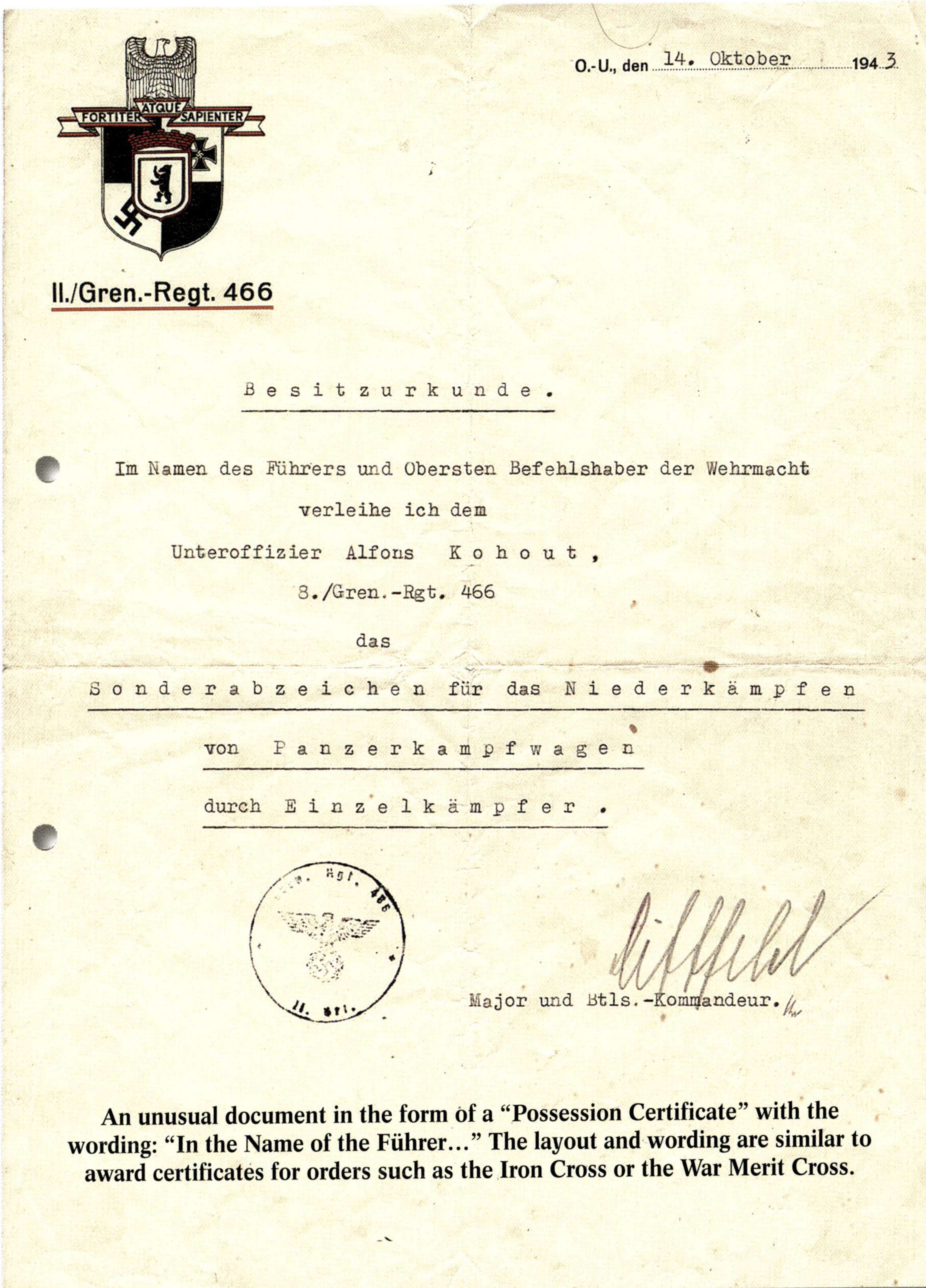

O.-U., den 14. Oktober 1943

II./Gren.-Regt. 466

FORTITER ATQUE SAPIENTER

Besitzurkunde.

Im Namen des Führers und Obersten Befehlshaber der Wehrmacht

verleihe ich dem

Unteroffizier Alfons Kohout,

8./Gren.-Rgt. 466

das

Sonderabzeichen für das Niederkämpfen

von Panzerkampfwagen

durch Einzelkämpfer.

Major und Btls.-Kommandeur.

An unusual document in the form of a "Possession Certificate" with the wording: "In the Name of the Führer…" The layout and wording are similar to award certificates for orders such as the Iron Cross or the War Merit Cross.

A rare type of possession certificate for the Tank Destruction Badge.

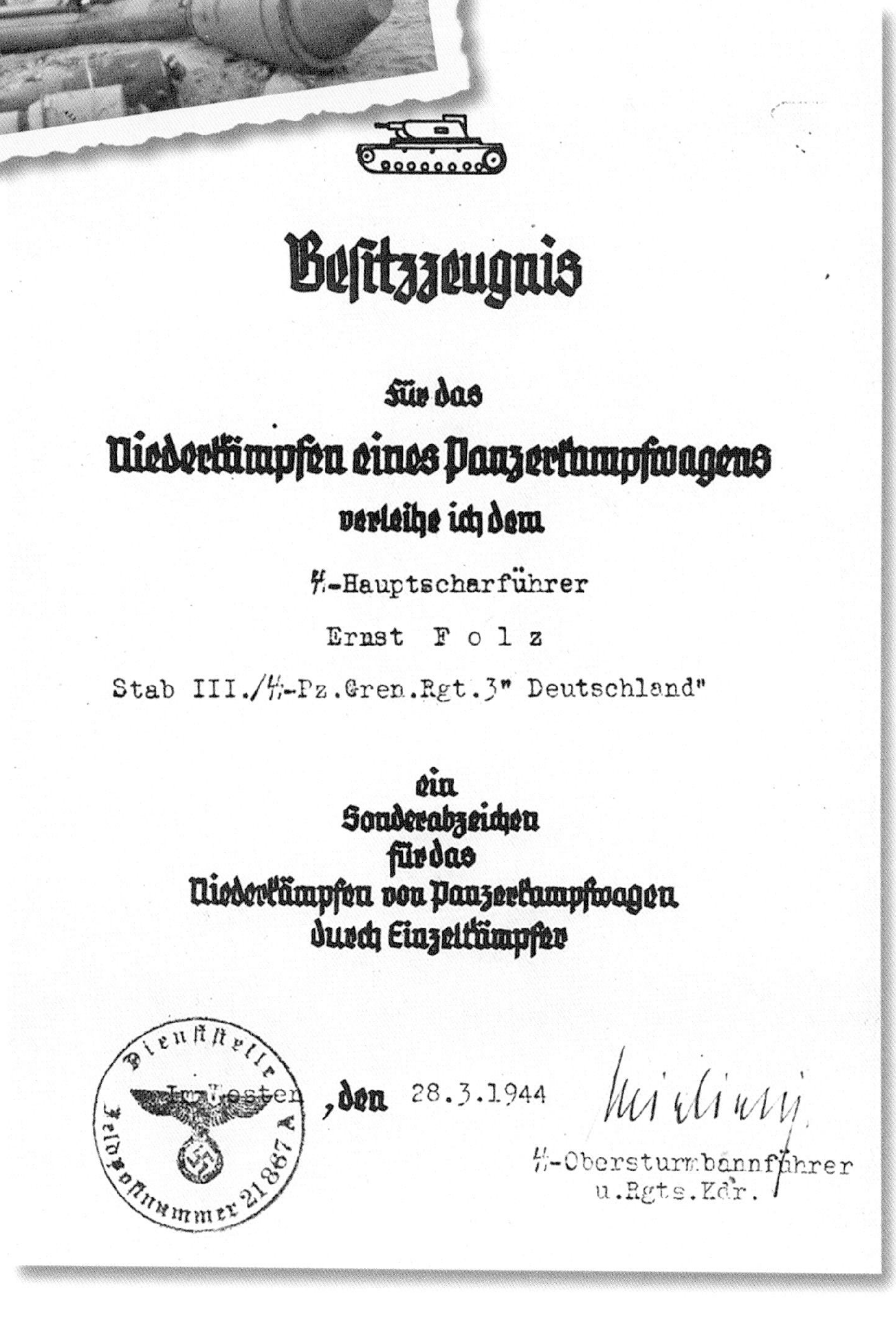

Besitzzeugnis

für das

Niederkämpfen eines Panzerkampfwagens

verleihe ich dem

SS-Hauptscharführer

Ernst F o l z

Stab III./SS-Pz.Gren.Rgt.3" Deutschland"

ein

Sonderabzeichen

für das

Niederkämpfen von Panzerkampfwagen

durch Einzelkämpfer

Dienststelle Feldpostnummer 21867 A

Im Westen ,den 28.3.1944

[signature]

SS-Obersturmbannführer
u.Rgts.Kdr.

"Pionier-Oberfeldwebel, accomplished in close-range attacks against tanks."

A typical propaganda postcard by W. Willrich.

Both of these soldiers wear the Close Combat Bar.
The Unteroffizier on the left also wears two Tank Destruction Badges.

Oberleutnant d.R. Hans-Georg Borck (Knight's Cross on 23/12/43) singlehandedly destroyed four tanks.

Oberleutnant Bodo Spranz (Knight's Cross with Oak Leaves on 3/10/43) also destroyed four tanks in close-range combat.

In this photo Hauptmann Hans-Gustav Jochims (Knight's Cross on 19/9/43) is also wearing four Tank Destruction Badges.

Training

Like almost everything in the German military, the close-range engagement of tanks was also regulated by an Army Service Manual (Heeresdienstvorschrift or HDV). In response to the dramatic developments on the Eastern Front, the Interim Guidelines for the Close-Range Engagement of Armored Vehicles (HDV 469/4) were issued on 29 January 1942. These were replaced by the Guidelines for the Close-Range Engagement of Armored Vehicles on 7 October 1942.

This final version of the army service manual covered close-range weapons as well as the training and organization of a so-called close-range anti-tank team (Panzernahkampftrupp). Its contents included:

— Tank recognition

— Use of close-range weapons

— Attacking a stationary tank

— Engaging an attacking tank

— Destroying a moving tank

— Defending against a surprise tank attack

— Engaging an attacking tank with defending mounted infantry

— Engaging tanks approaching to attack

Whereas this service manual was intended to be a guide for the instructors of so-called "close-range anti-tank teams" (later called "tank-destroyer teams"), Instructional Pamphlet 77/3, which was issued on 13 May 1944, was aimed directly at the individual soldiers engaged in close-range combat against enemy tanks. Aptly named "The Tank Cracker", it was intended to supplement the soldier's previous training.

This instructional pamphlet is reproduced in its entirety in the appendix. It provides a wealth of information, and therefore will only be addressed tangentially in the subsequent text.

This Gefreiter of the Luftwaffe anti-aircraft artillery, who wears the specialty badge of the anti-aircraft sound locater personnel, demonstrates the use of the Faustpatrone 30 "Gretchen."

Use of the Panzerfaust (klein) 30.

In the top photo, members of a headquarters staff, knowing that they will probably never find themselves in a situation requiring the use of a panzerfaust in earnest, display lukewarm interest as an Oberleutnant demonstrates how to use the weapon.

Likewise in the bottom two photos, the grenadiers show little enthusiasm for their demonstration.

The Wehrpass of a member of the 6th Panzer Army who, in March 1945, attended a two-day close-range anti-tank course on the Panzerfaust 60.

Anti-Tank Weapons and Devices

Tanks could be engaged both at close quarters and from a distance. German soldiers had a variety of resources at their disposal, some of them improvised. The army service manual subdivided the close-range resources into:

— Blinding Devices, which were used to force moving tanks to stop. The most important of these were the purposely-developed Blendkörper 1 H and 2 H, plus smoke generators, smoke, and covering the vision slits with mud or tent quarters.

— Destructive Devices, which in turn were subdivided into:

1.) Flame Devices, which were supposed to be used against vision slits or engine openings. The most important of these were gasoline bombs, flamethrowers or a smoke grenade attached to a gasoline can.

2.) Explosive Devices. The most important of these were:

a. Hafthohlladung 3 and 3.5 kg. (hollow charge magnetic mines). Their tremendous blast and sound pressure effects made them the most effective close-range anti-tank weapons. The charge was placed on the tank by hand and held there by a magnetic tripod. The charges were equipped with time fuses with a delay of 4½ seconds and later 7 seconds. As the soldier had to be in direct contact with the tank and, provided he was not operating from his foxhole, had to approach the tank without being seen, this was also the most dangerous method of disabling a tank.

b. T-Mine 35 and 43. These mines weighed approximately 10 kg (5 kg of which was explosives) and were about 32 cm in diameter. They could either be placed directly on the tank between the turret and hull or, in more common practice, laid as a mine barrier. In the latter case they were buried 8 – 10 cm deep. In sandy soil the mines could be buried up to 15 cm deep. The rotary safety switch was set to "scharf" (armed) prior to placement of the mine and the arming wire of the safety pin was supposed to indicate "freundwarts" (friendward). The mines detonated at a pressure load of 210 kg and, like the hollow charge magnetic mine, had the same penetrative ability as the solid-core armor-piercing round of the Pak 40 at a range of 100 meters.

c. Hand Grenades, which were lobbed individually into hatches or openings or used in so-called concentrated charges. These concentrated charges consisted of the heads of seven stick grenades held together with wire. The weapon had no penetrative power but was capable of temporarily deafening the crew of the tank.

Among the (close-range) anti-tank weapons that could be employed from a certain distance were:

1. Panzerbüchsen (Anti-tank Rifles). Conceived as super-heavy rifles to counter Allied tanks at the end of the First World War. From them evolved the Panzerbüchse 38, which weighed about 16 kg and was 1.615 mm in length. It was capable of penetrating 30 mm or armor at a range of 100 m. This was reduced to 20 mm at a range of 300 m. The Panzerbüchse 39 was subsequently introduced, with a reduced weight of just under 13 kg. Both had a caliber of 7.92 mm and were virtually useless by the time of the Western Campaign in 1940. In an effort to prolong their service lives, rifle discharger cups were added to both weapons, turning them into grenade launchers. Despite their lack of accuracy, both weapons remained in service with some units until 1944. Introduced in June 1940, the schwere Panzerbüchse 41 fired 28-mm armor-piercing or high-explosive ammunition. It was capable of penetrating approx. 60 mm of armor from a range of 100 m and 25 mm from 1000 m. The new anti-tank rifle was 2850 mm long with a barrel length of 1700 mm. Weight, including removable wheels, was 147 kg. In firing position it still weighed 137 kg. Average usable range rose to 500 m. A total of about 1,600 Panzerbüchsen 38 were made, plus just under 40,000 Panzerbüchsen 39 and about 2,700 schwere Panzerbüchsen 41. The actual cost of the latter was about 4,500 Reichsmark!

2. Panzerfäuste. After it was shown that the anti-tank rifles used by grenadiers and the 37- and 50-mm anti-tank guns (abbreviated Pak – ultimately referred to sarcastically as tank door knockers) were ineffective against the tanks fielded by the Soviets and the western allies, in the summer of 1942 development began of a so-called Faustpatrone based on the principle of the hollow charge. Like the hollow charge magnetic mine, the top part of the projectile was hollow, with the explosives (a mixture of TNT and Trihexogen – 400 grams in the Panzerfaust 30 and 800 grams in the larger versions) in the lower part. The charge's funnel shape concentrated the gases produced by the explosion in one place, melting the armor there. The recoilless—open in the rear—weapon consisted of an 80-cm-long tube, into which was inserted a round with a diameter of 100 mm. This round was attached to a wooden rod fitted with metal fins. Overall length was just under 50 cm. The fins were supposed to provide a more stable flight path, but in fact most projectiles "wobbled" toward their target. The first such weapon was introduced in 1943 as the Faustpatrone 30 and was capable of penetrating 140 mm of steel at a distance of about 30 meters. From it was developed the Panzerfaust 30 (klein), a somewhat modified version. Approaching to within 30 meters of

the target still placed the user in great danger, therefore an attempt was made to increase firing range by increasing the size of the propellant charge. As a result, the tube had to be strengthened somewhat. Introduced in mid-1944, the Panzerfaust 60 could be fired from a distance of about 60 meters. To improve its penetrative ability, the explosive charge was increased in diameter to 150 mm. The modified round was capable of penetrating approximately 200 mm of steel. Another improvement in range was achieved with the Panzerfaust 100, which was introduced in November 1944. It used a new propellant charge which enabled the round to achieve the necessary speed. Finally the Panzerfaust 150 was produced, also by modifying the propellant charge, and it enabled a soldier to fire at a tank from a distance of about 150 meters. Accuracy began to suffer with the Panzerfaust 60 and 100 and many shots simply missed the target. Placing chicken wire on a tank provided a simple solution to the panzerfaust, significantly reducing the effectiveness of the warhead. Weighing barely 7 kg (the Panzerfaust 30 weighed just over 3 kg), it was, however, an easy-to-use and immensely practical weapon. The relationship between the almost ten million Panzerfausts produced (approx. three million Panzerfaust 30, six million Panzerfaust 60, two million Panzerfaust 100 and about 100,000 Panzerfaust 150) and the number of tanks disabled by them (about 15,000) does, however, illustrate the surprising ineffectiveness of this anti-tank weapon.

3. Raketen-Panzerbüchsen (anti-tank rocket launchers). Inspired by captured American bazookas, in the spring of 1943 development began of an anti-tank rocket launcher, which in the soldier's jargon was referred to as the "Tank Terror" or "Stovepipe". With a caliber of 88 mm, it weighed 9.25 kg and 1640 mm long. In contrast to the panzerfausts, it could be reloaded repeatedly by its two-man crew. The projectile weighed 3.25 kg, had a 660-gram hollow charge and was fin stabilized. Initially the operator wore a gas mask to protect him against the flame jet. Later a 36 x 47 cm protective shield was mounted, making the gas mask unnecessary. With shield, the weapon weighed about 11 kg and could be fired from a distance of about 150 m. A total of about 300,000 anti-tank rocket launchers (8,8 cm RPzB 54) were made at a unit price of about 70 Reichsmark (total cost about 21 million Reichsmark). In his previously-cited study[3], Hans Jürgen Pantenius wrote: "The anti-tank defense was completely inadequate. For technical reasons the infantry guns were only a stopgap, furthermore the purpose of an infantry gun was completely different from that of an anti-tank gun. The anti-tank rocket launcher, also called "Panzerschreck", had a tube diameter of 88 mm and a projectile capable of penetrating all known tanks. Its combat range of about 200 m was quite inadequate, furthermore the almost

---

3 Pantenius, Hans Jürgen: Letzte Schlacht an der Ostfront, Hamburg 2002

Wrecked tanks.

three-meter-long flame jet from the back end of the tube betrayed the position of the two operators. In open terrain this meant the immediate destruction of the crew. Use of the weapon was only practical in towns and forests. As training on the weapon was relatively simple and required no particular knowledge, I disbanded the (anti-tank rocket launcher) company there and then and assigned the platoons to the battalions. The company was not employable as a self-contained unit anyway."

Panzerbüchse 38

Panzerbüchse 39

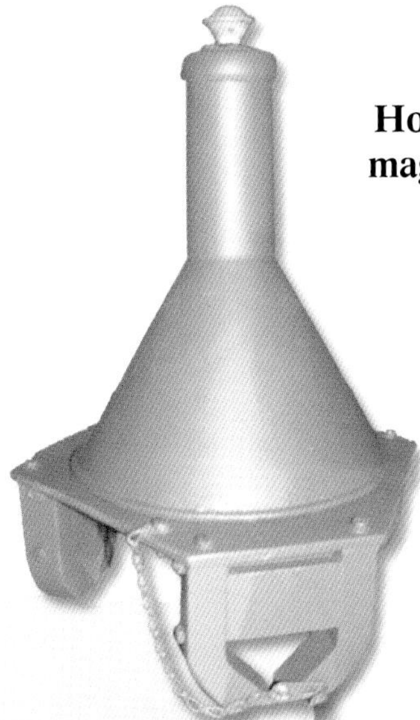

Hollow charge magnetic mine.

Until the panzerfaust entered service, the hollow charge magnetic mine was the most important close-range anti-tank weapon. It remained in use even in 1944/45. In the photo below, members of the Volksstum are familiarized with its use.

Soldier with a Tellermine 43.

Tellermine 35.

Knocked-out M4 Sherman tank.

Faustpatrone 30
"Gretchen".

SS-Oberscharführer Thurner, a member of the SS Anti-Tank Battalion "Das Reich", was awarded the German Cross in Gold on 8/9/43. He also wears a Tank Destruction Badge.

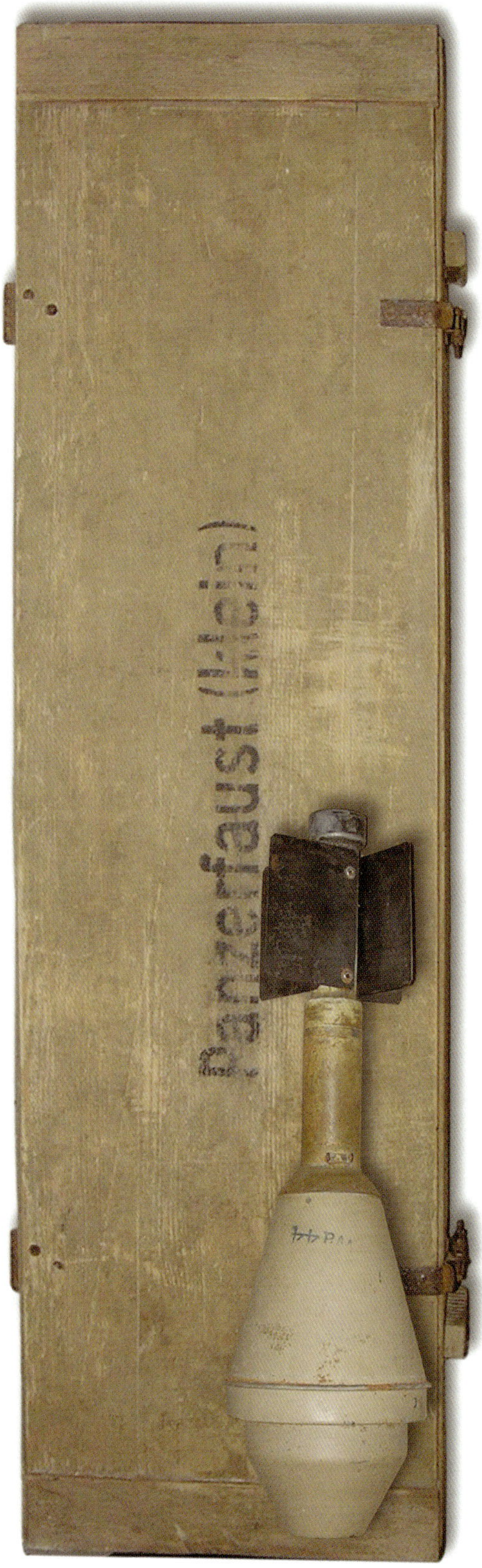

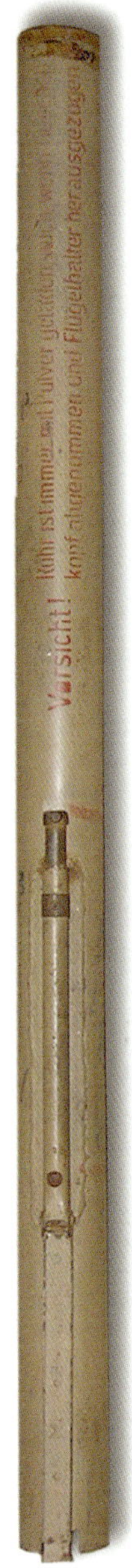

Panzerfaust (Klein) 30

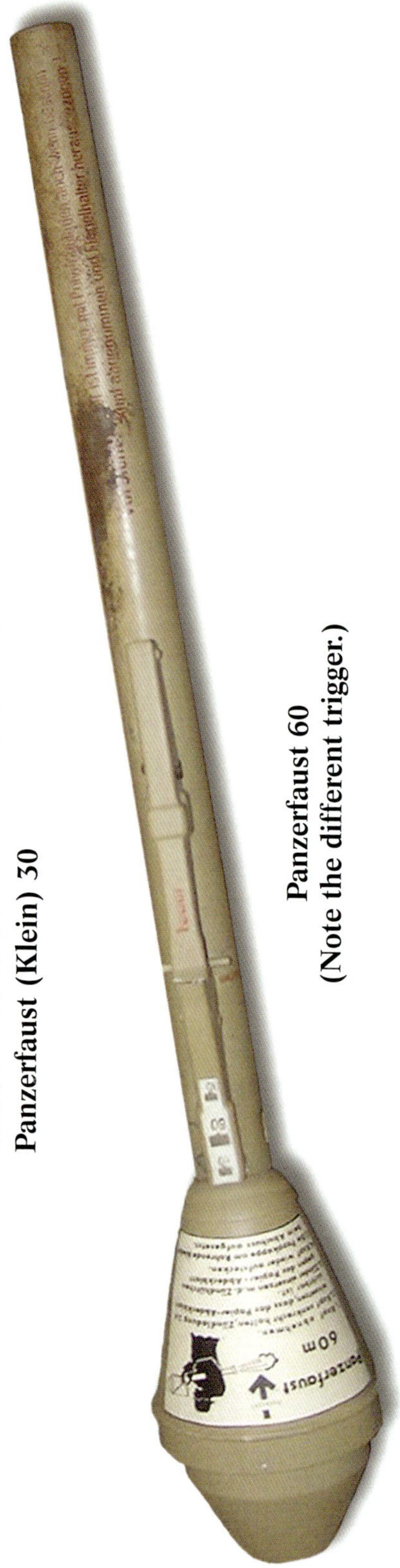

Panzerfaust 60
(Note the different trigger.)

Raketen-Panzerbüchse 54

Metal blast shield

When the blast shield was not present (above right), the operator wore his gas mask to protect himself against the rocket exhaust gases.

Recollections

H. Findeisen remembers using hollow charge magnetic mines in 1942:

> "When we marched into Russia, we had no answer to the enemy's heavy tanks. Our 37- and 50-mm anti-tank guns barely damaged them and one by one they were simply overrun. When we were encircled at Demyansk our only option was to attack the tanks from close range. The way we did this was to observe which routes the Russian tanks took during an attack. The Russians constantly repeated their attacks and they often followed the same route in order to avoid minefields. We dug tank defense holes in these lanes, staggered from the main line of resistance into the rear. When the enemy attacked, a comrade slipped into each of these holes with one or two hollow charge magnetic mines. I did it too…my greatest fear was that the tank driver would see my hole and begin spinning the tank over top of it, or that I would set the mine to explode but then the tank wouldn't move any farther!
>
> Near the front we received a quick briefing from pioneers on how to use hollow charge magnetic mines. This included the best place to attach it to the bottom of the tank. Unlike the sides, which were heavily armored, the undersides of the tank were weakly protected. The hollow charge magnetic mine worked like a welding torch and if it struck ammunition inside the tank it could cause it to explode. During the demonstration by the pioneers, they lit a hollow charge magnetic mine and we could really hear it hiss.
>
> Sometimes those who waited in the holes for the enemy tanks received some sort of benefit even without having destroyed a tank, as they had exhibited conspicuous bravery. If an enemy tank was engaged successfully, in the beginning there was the Iron Cross and/or some leave, and then later the so-called Tank Destruction Sleeve Band. Although I waited in a hole for my chance several times, I wasn't able to destroy any tanks. A number of my comrades, however, succeeded several times."

In late 1943 – early 1944, Leo Wilm destroyed two Soviet T-34s:

> "At the end of 1943, during its winter offensive, the Red Army once again broke through the German positions and our peaceful days were over. We were loaded onto trucks and sent into the Krivoy Rog area, where all hell had broken loose. There was much hand-to-hand fighting, and we succeeded in holding our positions. When the enemy pulled back a little, I was given the task of reconnoitering a village situated in front of us.

At first all was quiet, but then there was a sudden outburst of heavy machine-gun and mortar fire. While my boys and I were still lying on the ground, a Soviet tank came rattling towards us. It halted about 30 meters away, its side facing me. I called for a panzerfaust and aimed just below the turret. At first the tank poured smoke, then there was a big explosion that blew the turret off the hull. The hollow charge round had probably detonated armor-piercing ammunition in the turret. Taking advantage of the confusion, we ran back to our position. The village was obviously in enemy hands.

A few days later we took up positions in a forest near the Bessarabian border. While I was checking on my men to ensure that they all had good and secure positions, I heard tank noises. A lone T-34 came up a forest lane and stopped not far away. A hatch opened and a head appeared. As I couldn't see any more enemy tanks or infantry, I decided to knock out this tank too. I crawled towards it through the undergrowth and saw that two Red Army men had climbed out of the tank and were scanning the area. When I was sure I was in range, I fired the panzerfaust and hit the tank dead center.

The men of my platoon, some of whom were very young, watched this with wide eyes. They subsequently confirmed my account of these actions, and about 14 days later I was awarded two Special Badges for the Singlehanded Destruction of Tanks."

H. Lütjens knocked out an Allied tank in Normandy:

"On 11 June 1944 we were in the Brettville area. It was a warm morning and I was sitting in my foxhole writing a letter to my relatives. Suddenly Tommy opened up on the main line of resistance, which was about 200 meters away, with everything he had. As I hadn't been in action long, I became extremely uncomfortable. Suddenly my platoon leader shouted "tanks approaching", and to me, "Lütjens, panzerfaust, go!". I had been taught that detonators and explosives were always to be kept separate, and there we were! W. Stinner, who was about 20 meters away in his foxhole, had the panzerfaust detonators. Meanwhile the tanks drew ever closer. My platoon leader continued urging me: "Lütgens, go, take the first tank!". Summoning my courage, I climbed out of my hole and crawled over to W. Stinner. He tossed them to me and called, "Good luck!" I crawled back to my hole, grabbed the first of the three panzerfausts lying there and armed it. Then I searched for my victim. There it was, big and powerful, a Sherman. I began crawling towards it. When I was 20 meters away I squeezed the trigger—but nothing happened. I cocked and tried again—but again nothing. Not until the third try did the round fire. I didn't see the impact as the other tanks opened fire on me. I did hear an explosion, then I raced back to my hole, zigzagging the whole way. Then, suddenly, the Tommies turned back. I soon realized why: three German assault guns had joined the battle. The order to counterattack came as a relief. When the powder smoke had cleared, I examined "my" tank. I had hit it in front, right over the driver's seat. The projectile had welded its way through the spare track and armor. Suddenly the battalion commander was standing beside me: "Thanks very much Lütjens, the fellow was making things hot for us! He was just about to open fire on my bunker, and who knows what would have happened if he had taken it out." He presented me with an Iron Cross, Second Class and assured me that he was going to put me up for the Special Badge for the Singlehanded Destruction of Tanks. I was 17 years old."

K. Hess was also a 17-year-old when he engaged a Soviet tank in East Prussia in the autumn of 1944:

"We were transferred to East Prussia in the autumn of 1944. Our final stop was Insterburg. From there it was another 17 km to Gumbinnen, where elements of the "Hermann Göring" Parachute-Panzer Corps were quartered in the barns and stables of the Zweilinden estate. The rumble of guns could be heard in the distance. Thirty-three men, including me, were called out by name and the next day we were put on trucks and assigned to the parachute-panzer corps' assault battalion.

In the evening we moved forward through a wood to a trench which was already occupied by members of the army. One of them told me that all hell had been let loose there. Early that morning the Russians had broken through and had taken up position in another trench. We moved on through the trench and exited the forest. The next morning we saw the bodies of dead Russians littering the open areas.

Things stayed quiet for the next few days. One night we heard the sound of engines. Our squad leader, knowing they could only be coming from tanks, said that something wasn't right. The next day there was movement by the Russians. We opened fire with machine-guns and rifles, but after an hour everything became quiet again. Perhaps the enemy was merely testing us, trying to determine how strongly-manned our position was. Evening approached and we carefully scanned the terrain. At about two in the morning we again heard the sound of tank engines. I subsequently remarked to my squad leader that I wanted to have a go at one of the things.

The next night we heard the tank noises again, and I told my comrades not to shoot because I wanted to go down the slope a ways. I collected six hand grenades, a pistol and a panzerfaust and set out. I came to a tree and saw that someone was lying to the right of it. With my pistol ready, I moved closer. The head was facing east, as if he was observing. I nudged the body with my foot. There was no movement. To be sure, I struck the head hard with the toe of my boot and realized that he was dead. Then I lay down to the left of the tree. I made the hand grenades ready to throw, the panzerfaust ready to fire and placed the pistol where I could reach it. When it slowly began to get dark, the tank began moving toward me. When I saw that there were several figures sitting on the tank, I became nervous. Before they saw me, I fired the panzerfaust and threw a few hand grenades at them. Then I took to my heels. After a few meters I turned around and saw that the tank was spinning on its axis, and so I ran back. The hand grenades had probably taken care of the escorting infantry. I climbed onto the tank and found an open hatch. I armed another hand grenade, counted to 23 and dropped the thing inside. Then I ran back up the slope and let myself fall into our trench. I was so terribly excited that I almost failed to notice the congratulations of my comrades."

G. Adam and a comrade destroyed a T-34 on 2 February 1945:

"The Red Army had outflanked us near Neu-Bentschen on 20 January 1945 and we were in a small pocket. Under indescribable conditions we, a scratch unit made up of men from NCO schools and officer candidate courses, tried to break out to the west to regain out lines. After several fierce battles, there wasn't much left of our once quite formidable battle group.

Everywhere there was lack of discipline and signs of disintegration. Officers and NCOs had removed their rank badges and everyone was trying to get through to the west any way they could.

My platoon stayed together and during the night of 1-2 February 1945 we came upon two Landesschütze (regional defense) sentries in a wood. They told us that their job was to tell us how to get to the Oder. They said we were close to Gr. Blumberg on the Oder. There was no enemy in the town and we were expected. Soon afterwards there appeared a Hauptmann, who was directed in exactly the opposite direction. Suspicious, we questioned the two men and concluded that they were members of the National Committee for a Free Germany. The Hauptmann subsequently drew the necessary conclusions...

During the night we came to some houses, from which we drew fire. There was shooting from everywhere. A Vierlingsflak that had joined us a short time earlier opened fire, blazing away into the village. We began our breakthrough and found that there were Russians everywhere. The entire village street was full of panye wagons and other vehicles. I told my people to shoot at the windows and also to lob hand grenades or captured Russian infantry mines inside. Suddenly a T-34 appeared from behind the last house at the end of the street. Its barrel swung in our direction and spat out shot after shot without regard for the Russian soldiers. Each shell blasted pieces of panye wagon into the air. Horses were hit and lay thrashing about on the street.

I took cover behind the small stone steps of one of the houses and Feldwebel Speck kneeled behind me. It was clear that the tank had to go, and I had Speck pass me a panzerfaust. I also took an infantry mine.

Advancing on the tank was hell. We could have been taken out by a tank shell at any moment, for the T-34 was still firing completely randomly down the street. As we neared it, it suddenly moved forward, exposing its broadside! And that was its undoing. Speck's panzerfaust struck it dead center and my mine exploded on its right track, causing it to come off. Amidst the smoke a hatch opened, but to no avail. Jubilant German infantry shot the crew with rifles as they baled out.

Now the Russians were running away everywhere. Before us lay the riverbank and beyond the frozen Oder. From the other side flares rose into the sky, showing us the way across the ice. As soon as we reached the other side my men suddenly took off. They wanted to get back to their own units or "home to mother" as quickly as possible. A police unit equipped with old 08/15 machine-guns, with which they intended or were supposed to prevent the Russians from crossing the Oder, directed me on to Rothenburg on the Oder. On 3 March 1945 Speck and I were awarded the Badge for the Singlehanded Destruction of Tanks."

A former member of SS Assault Brigade "Dirlewanger" remembered his training on the panzerfaust and the destruction of a T-34 during the street fighting in Sommerfeld in February 1945:

"Training of the new men resumed--marching, rifle practice and, in particular, instruction on the panzerfaust. An Oberscharführer arrived with two men and about 15 panzerfausts. Until then I had only fired the panzerfaust twice, in Warsaw. They explained the procedure: pull the safety pin, raise the folding sight and aim through the three aiming slots (range estimation required), how to hold the weapon on the shoulder when firing from a prone, kneeling or standing position or under the arm from a kneeling or standing position. They emphasized that no one should be behind the tube when the weapon was fired, otherwise burns could result from the flame jet produced by the propellant charge. We were supposed to aim between the turret and hull of a tank, but that was hardly ever possible. Aiming was so inaccurate that one either had to get to within a few meters or simply aim roughly and fire. The projectile had a range of about 100 meters, but at that range a hit on the target was pure luck. The best range was 40 meters or less. How to hit anything beyond that was a mystery to me. After about an hour's training in a nearby field, we fired the 15 panzerfausts. The target was a tree about 40 meters away. Of the 15 projectiles only one hit the tree. Three landed nearby, the others were scattered all over the place. The propellant charge of one panzerfaust even failed to ignite. In any case, my shot landed only about two meters from the tree and I was more or less satisfied. Afterwards the men ridiculed this wonder weapon, which was also not surprising...

When we retook Sommerfeld in street and house fighting, a member of my company drew my attention to two approaching T-34s. They immediately began shooting at us. The window frame fell out, the plaster crumbled and in addition to a lot of smoke, fire broke out. We ducked our heads and considered what to do. First the tanks had to go. I said to my two runners: "Let's go, two panzerfausts each and follow me." We made our way down the wooden stairs from the second floor and ran to the ground floor window. Several members of my company were already huddled there. The two tanks were sitting on the street off to the right, taking turns firing into the houses. From that angle, while we could see them, aiming and shooting with the panzerfaust was impossible. To step out into the street would have been suicide, so we waited. Then, all of a sudden, the engines roared, the tracks rattled and one of the tanks began to move. It advanced hesitantly and stopped after a few meters. But that was enough for me to be able to take aim. I instructed one of my runners to go to the window behind me and keep watch to prevent Ivan from shooting me, while I gave the other my submachine-gun so that he could shoot any of the crew that might get out. Then I took the safety off, raised the sight, aimed at the tank—which was perhaps 30 meters away—and pressed down on the lever. Trailing fire, the projectile flew towards the tank and struck it. As I watched tensely, it began to smoke heavily and then there was an explosion. I quickly ducked my head and then peered again through the empty window. The thing was still sitting there but not moving. I had knocked out a Russian tank. That was on the afternoon of 22 February 1945. Several days later I was ordered to report to SS-Hauptsturmführer Momm who, with a brief "Here, congratulations", handed me a sleeve band for the destruction of a tank. "Go to the senior NCO and have him enter the decoration in your paybook."

H. Draeger's account includes a description of how a panzerfaust was used in hand-to-hand combat. He was wounded while attempting to destroy a Stalin tank:

"The 12th of February 1945 began with a mortar barrage by the Russians. Lying in a forest under mortar fire is extremely unpleasant. The shells exploded in the treetops, showering the troops below with fragments. We all put on our steel helmets, nevertheless there were numerous head wounds. The Russians attacked but were beaten off. Indian-like, the Russians crawled up to our positions, suddenly rose up and, screaming their "Urrah" war cry, were upon us. We were all veteran soldiers and Russian attacks didn't shake us. We even used the panzerfaust in a way that was never intended. In hand-to-hand combat the fiery trail immediately created breathing space!

Then a Russian tank felt its way down the road. I and my company headquarters squad leader immediately left our position and moved forward. We each had a panzerfaust. Suddenly I heard a dull thump. My company headquarters squad leader had fired his panzerfaust. I saw the projectile pass over the tank. Aha, I thought to myself, if you estimated 80 meters, I'll try 60. I was right and my panzerfaust projectile hit the target. The track below the turret was damaged and the tank could no longer move. We crawled back and I reported what had happened to battalion.

Then the Russians sent another tank, a type I had never seen before. I later learned that it was a Stalin. Apparently this giant was supposed to recover the damaged tank. Again my company headquarters squad leader tried to get close to the tank, but this time the Soviets were on the alert. We came under submachine-gun fire, immediately withdrew and decided to try again from the other side of the road.

I took another man, W. Birke, to provide covering fire and entered the forest on the right side of the road. Unable to find a good firing position, we pulled back again. Just before the edge of the forest in the direction of the open fields outside Grabow, I heard a rifle shot and turned around. Lying in the ditch, my escort had used his sniper rifle to shoot a Russian fiddling with the knocked-out tank. As I turned my head I saw the turret of the Stalin tank rotating in our direction. I saw a flash from the muzzle of the gun, heard a bang, saw fire nearby and fell to the ground. I knew at once that I had been hit. My first instinct was to get up and run for cover. But my legs wouldn't work, and so I pulled myself behind a small rise. When I felt my pants with my hands, I thought: Shit, now your legs are gone.

The high-explosive shell from the tank had flown into the forest and exploded against a tree behind me. The splinter effect was so great that all three of us were on the ground even though there we were separated by at least forty paces. We called over to the company and an infantryman came running. I instructed him to summon the Leutnant, who was positioned at the edge of the forest with three assault guns, so that we could be recovered under their protection.

The infantryman returned and said that the Leutnant had denied my request, as he had to remain in an ambush position and wait for a possible attack by Russian tanks. Our battalion was then advised and they replied that we would be recovered when darkness fell. We were wounded at about 14:30!

While we waited on the frozen ground the Russians shelled us with mortars. I was wounded again, in the right thigh and in the nose. Then, in the evening, two motorcycle-sidecar combinations with mounted stretchers arrived. That's how we were evacuated."

A. Ruf, a member of the Hitler Youth, saw an American tank knocked out during the final battles in Nuremberg:

"When we 14- to 16-year-old Hitler Youths from the Nuremberg area were mobilized in April 1945 we were as proud as punch. Equipped with panzerfausts, we were supposed to become tank killers. In a wood to the northeast we came upon members of the SS who were only a little older than we. They were camped there and were armed to the teeth with infantry weapons. Unlike us, they had plenty of chocolate, which they generously shared. When American tanks approached Erlenstegen on 16 April 1945, we were ordered to the inner city. Of the poor guys who had stayed there and were supposed to stop the Amis, most had been killed. On 19 April 1945 the American troops reached the area around the citadel and Plärrer Square. There one of us knocked out an American tank with a panzerfaust. The tank was sitting astride the street, firing repeatedly at the citadel tower. Whether it suspected that there were German troops holed up there or simply wanted to destroy the tower I do not know. In any case, an approximately 15-year-old comrade set off with a panzerfaust and crawled up to the tank. He fired the panzerfaust and the tank began to smoke. It also immediately ceased firing and did not move again. When our excited comrade returned we gave him a joyous welcome. We were all excited and clapped him on the shoulder without stopping. The next day brought the end of the Battle of Nuremberg. Today I can say thank God!"

Pamphlet 77/3 – Manual for the Close-Range Tank Attacker, May 1944

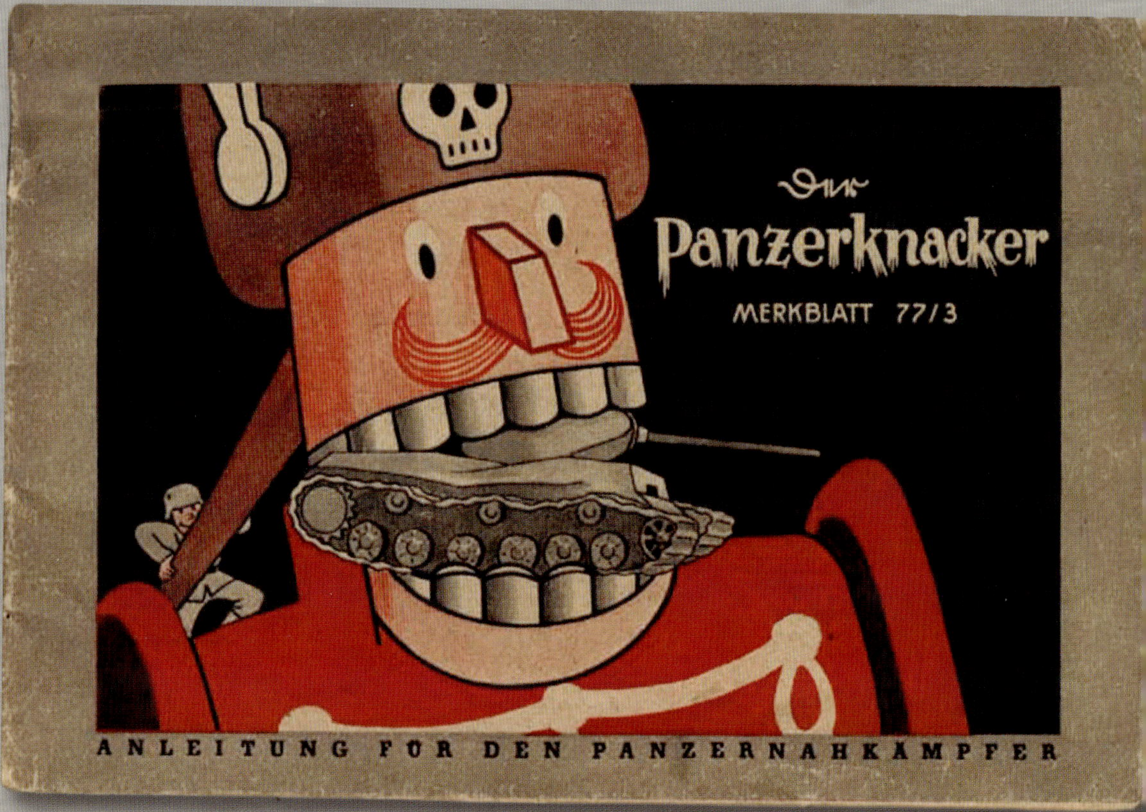

Auch Du....

... kannst Panzer knacken!

Schneid brauchst Du dazu und Geistesgegenwart, Vor allem aber siegt das überlegene Können!

Denk dran: Panzer kommen nicht nur dort, wo Pak steht. Alle Tage geschieht es, daß irgendwo Panzer durchsickern. Auch Du kannst plötzlich so einem Kasten gegenüberstehen. Jeder, ob beim Troß, ob im vordersten Graben, kommt einmal in diese Lage. Der Panzer fragt dann nicht, ob Du im Panzerknacken ausgebildet bist und als was.

Jeder kann das — **auch Du!**

1

These pages have been cleaned up for better readability.

Oberkommando des Heeres
Gen St d H / Der Panzeroffizier

H.Qu.OKH. den 13. Mai 1944

Das Merkblatt 77/3

„DER PANZERKNACKER"
(Anleitung für den Panzernahkämpfer)

vom 13. Mai 1944 ist zur Vertiefung der Ausbildung in der Panzernahbekämpfung an den einzelnen Soldaten auszugeben.

I. A.

v. GRUNDHERR

ALLE 150 METER EIN PANZER

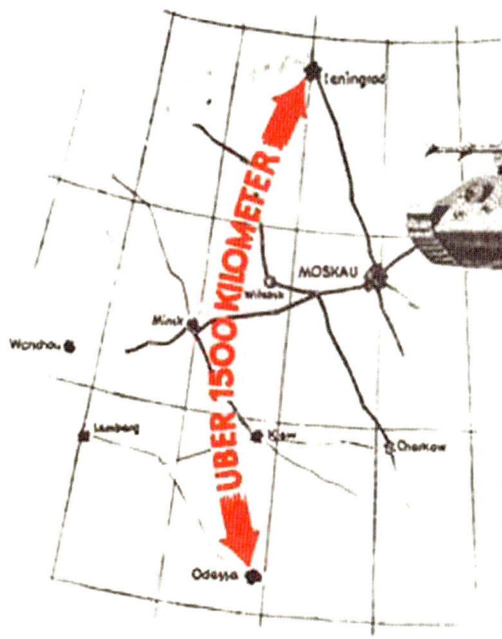

Was viele andre können täglich,
Das ist für Dich genau so möglich.

Über 10 000 deutsche Soldaten tragen das Panzernahkampf-Abzeichen. So viele geknackte Panzer entsprechen der Ausrüstung von 200 russischen Panzerbrigaden und der gesamten russischen Panzerproduktion in einem halben Jahr.

Und das alles nur mit den primitivsten Mitteln. Die aber lagen in der Hand von ganzen Kerlen, und darauf kommt's an.

Du fragst Dich, wie das möglich ist bei so ungleichen Bedingungen? Ganz klar: Erst einmal geht doch der Panzer auf gleichwertige Gegner los: Panzer, Pak und Flak. Von Dir will er zunächst gar nichts. Und dann, paß auf:

PANZER KNACKEN KANNST AUCH DU!

3

Dem stärksten Panzer selbst entsprechen
Auch andrerseits gewisse Schwächen.

Hast Du schon einmal zusammen mit Panzern angegriffen? Oder bist Du schon einmal in einem Panzer gesessen? Da wirst Du doch sofort bemerkt haben: Ganz so ungleich ist dieser Kampf, Männer gegen Panzer, gar nicht, denn

Auch ein Panzer hat seine Schwächen!

Er sieht schlecht, am schlechtesten das, was unmittelbar um ihn herum geschieht.

Er hört schlecht.

Er kann sich gegen Dich schlecht wehren, vor allem auf nächste Entfernung.

Er ist stark vom Gelände abhängig.

Die Schwächen der Panzer mußt Du kennen. Für jedes einzelne Baumuster findest Du sie haargenau in den Panzer-Nahkampftafeln (Anlagen zur H. Dv. 469/4). Laß sie Dir geben und studiere sie! **Die erste Forderung an den Panzerknacker ist: Typ erkennen! Schwächen wissen!** Dazu heißt's natürlich: beobachten, beobachten, beobachten!

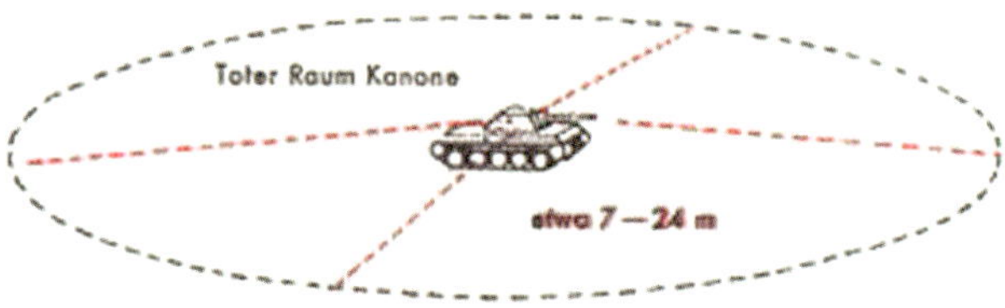

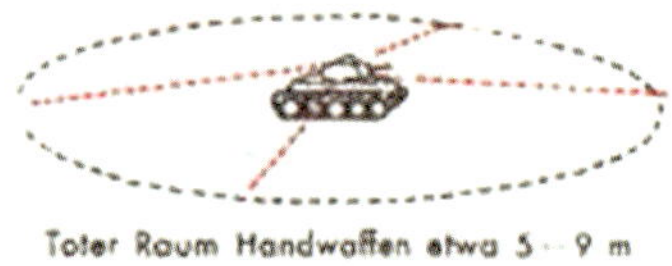

GEFÄHRLICHER ALS DER PANZER SELBST

Die Knackerei Erfolg verspricht,
Wenn Du die Schwächen kennst — sonst nicht.

Im großen merke Dir die schwachen Stellen nach dieser Skizze! Das ist aber nur eine schematische Zeichnung.

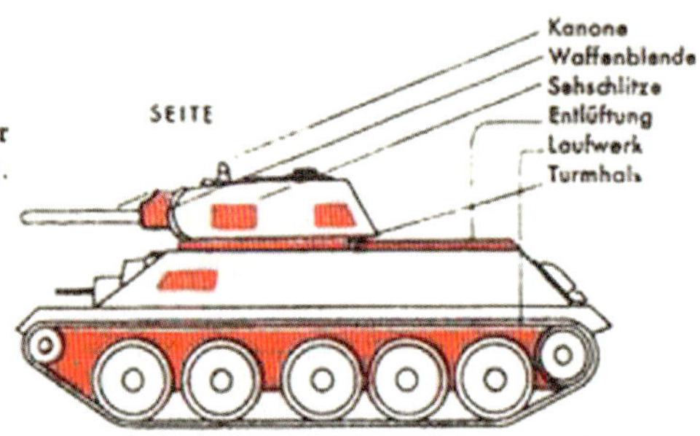

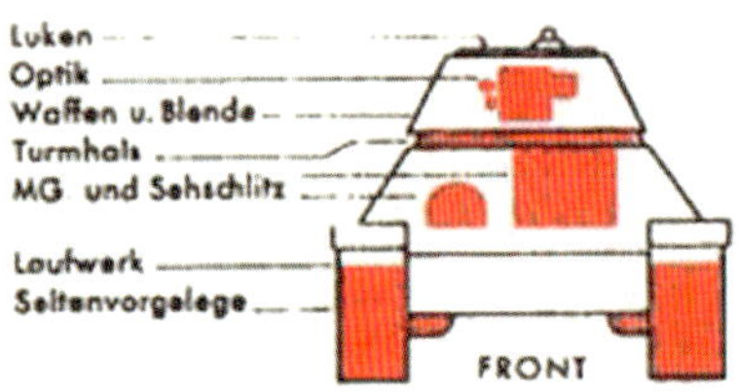

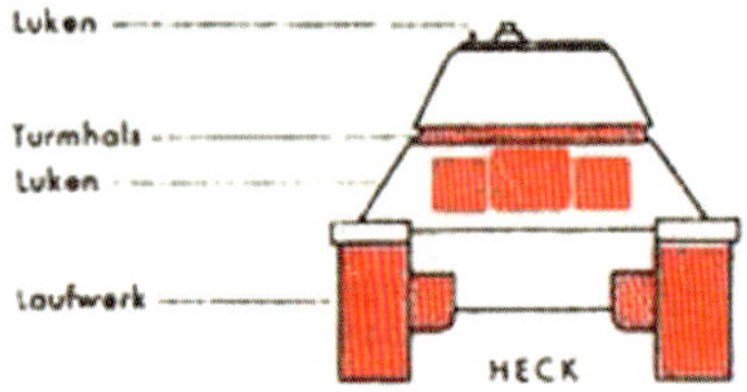

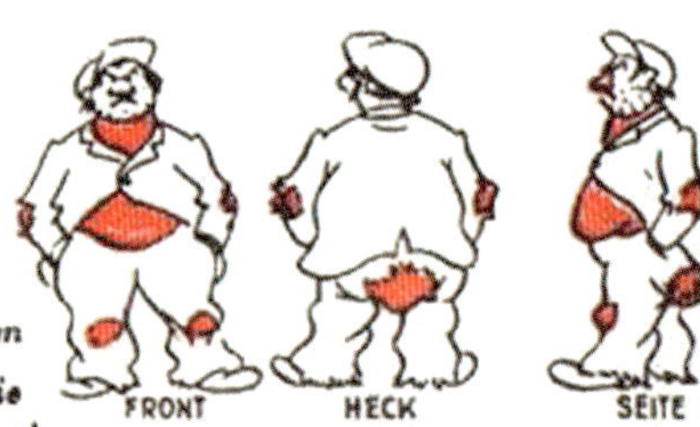

Sein Frack hat abgenützte Flächen
So zeigen auch die Panzer Schwächen!

Für die Lage dieser Stellen gibt's kein Grundrezept. Drum Panzer-Nahkampftafeln und Panzer-Erkennungstafeln einprägen!

IST DER SCHRECK, DEN ER ERZEUGT!

Diese wichtigsten Baumuster mußt Du sofort erkennen. Erst dann hat es Sinn, daß Du Dir ihre Schwächen einprägst.

Erst merke Dir den eleganten
Mit schrägen Flächen, runden Kanten,
5 Rollen, den studiere fleißig,
Denn das ist der **T 34.**

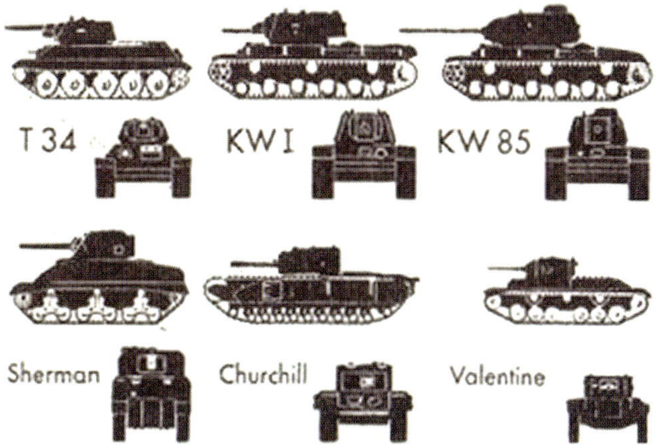

Von **KW I** ist dann zu sprechen,
Wenn scharfe Kanten, steile Flächen,
6 Rollen, massige Figur,
Des Wagens äußere Statur.

Gefährlich oft bemerkbar macht sich
Der starke **KW 85:**
Vom KW I das Fahrgestell,
Turm größer, runde Kanten, schnell.

Der **Sherman** ist, das sag ich ehrlich,
Von vorne gar nicht ungefährlich,
Ist ziemlich schnell, auch merk Dir ständig:
6 Rollen, runde Kanten, wendig.

Den **Churchill** wir erkennen sollen
An vielen, dafür kleinen Rollen,
Senkrechten Flächen. Er ist kläglich
Trotz großer Ketten unbeweglich.

Doch niedrige und schnelle Wagen,
Die zwei mal drei die Rollen tragen,
Das müssen **Valentinen** sein:
Das Tempo groß, die Stärke klein.

Sieh Dir die neuesten Panzer-Erkennungstafeln gründlich an! (Anl. zur H.Dv. 469/2a bzw. 2b.)

ERKENNEN AUF DEN ERSTEN BLICK!

Gefahren sind schon halb gebannt,
Sobald wir sie nur klar erkannt.

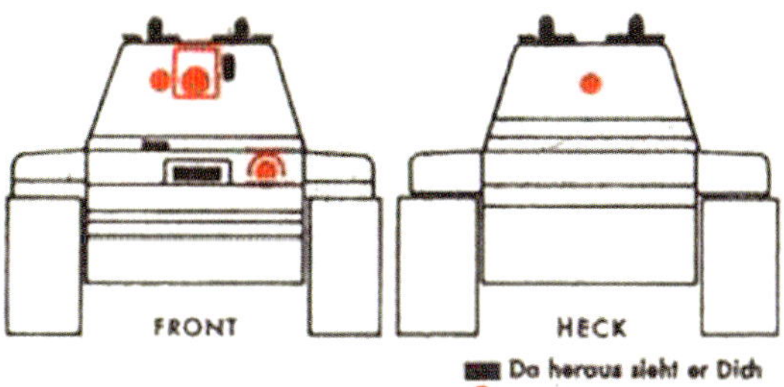

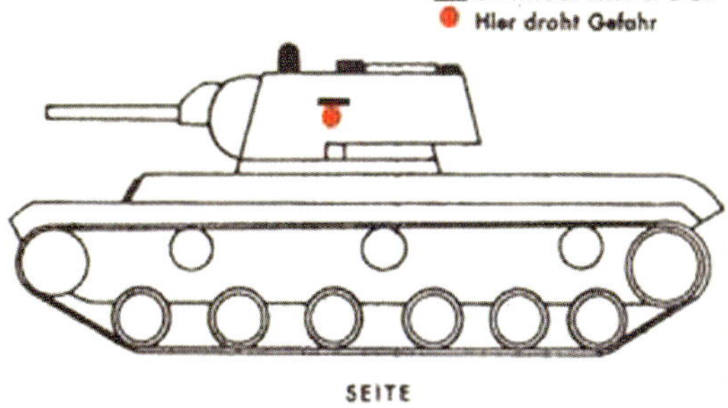

Ganz wehrlos gegen Nahangriff ist ein Panzer aber auch nicht. Er hat Nahkampföffnungen, durch die der Panzermann mit Pistolen und Maschinenpistolen schießt und durch die er Handgranaten werfen kann. Heck-MG. sind auch gefährlich. Du mußt nur wissen: Wo sieht er mich am leichtesten? Wo droht Gefahr?

Merke: Mit Handgranaten reicht er auch in den toten Raum hinein.

PASS AUF, HIER DROHT GEFAHR!

Gewicht ist nicht für Dich gefährlich,
Es ist vielmehr für ihn beschwerlich.

Jeder Panzer

muß halten, wenn er gezielt schießen will. Dann kommst aber auch Du viel leichter an ihn ran. Also: Wenn er's nicht von selber tut, zwing ihn zum Halten! Dabei sieh Dir erst das Gelände an! Denn jeder Panzer ist stark vom Gelände abhängig. Je schwerer, desto schwerfälliger ist er auch. In bedecktem Gelände wird seine schlechte Sicht noch schlechter. Also: Du mußt ihn dorthin locken, ihn da zum Halten bringen, wo Du die beste Deckung hast, er aber die größten Hindernisse. Sind von Natur aus keine da, dann mach' welche.

Diese Sperre kann natürlich keinem Panzer ein ernstes Hindernis sein. Aber sie hält ihn kurz auf, er muß langsam fahren, verliert den Überblick, und das ist Dein Moment. Jetzt kannst Du ihn knacken.

JE SCHWERER, DESTO SCHWERFÄLLIGER!

8

Daß man sie sich zunutze macht,
Sind schwache Stellen angebracht.

Halt!

Immer sachte. Erst mußt Du hier noch ein paar wichtige Dinge lernen. Ein Boxer, der auf Draht ist, der merkt nicht nur, wo der Gegner schwach ist, er nützt das auch aus und klotzt immer dorthin, wo er eine solche Stelle entdeckt hat. Mach's genau so!

Du weißt, er sieht schlecht. Also nicht rühren. Wer läuft, stirbt. Übrigens kannst Du ihm seine schlechte Sicht sogar noch ganz nehmen. Dazu hast Du Blendmittel. Schieß außerdem mit Handwaffen auf Schlitze und Optik. Auch mit der Leuchtpistole. Das ist nachts besonders wirkungsvoll. Wenn der Panzer steht, sind Schlitze gar nicht schwer zu treffen.

Daß er schlecht hört, das kommt Dir bei der Verständigung mit Deinen Kameraden zugute. Aber wenn der Motor nicht läuft, sei darin vorsichtig!

Du weißt, er kann sich auf nächste Entfernung schlecht wehren. Am sichersten bist Du also im toten Raum. Drum noch einmal: Wer läuft, stirbt. Wenn Du keinen Panzerschreck, keine Panzerfaust hast, dann mußt Du ja ohnehin ganz an den Kerl rankommen. Seine wenigen Nahkampföffnungen kannst Du leicht im Auge behalten.

W E R L Ä U F T , S T I R B T !

9

Mit Schneid und Deinen Nahkampfwaffen
Wirst Du den stärksten Panzer schaffen.

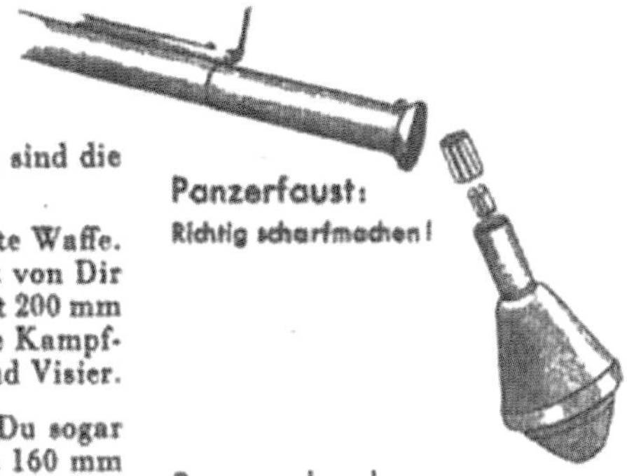

Panzerfaust:
Richtig scharfmachen!

Deine Stärke ist Mut und Entschlossenheit. Deine Waffen sind die besten, die es heute gibt:

Vor allem hast Du die **Panzerfaust.** Sie ist Deine wichtigste Waffe. Sie spart Dir das Anpirschen an den Panzer. Sie verlangt von Dir nur kaltes Blut. Alles andere tut sie selber. Sie durchschlägt 200 mm Panzerung und trifft sicher, wenn Du nur sauber zielst. Die Kampfentfernung Deiner Panzerfaust steht deutlich auf Kopf und Visier.

Fast ebenso einfach ist der **Panzerschreck.** Damit kannst Du sogar noch weiter vom Panzer entfernt bleiben. Er durchschlägt 160 mm Panzerung und trifft bis auf 150 m.

Panzerschreck:
Granate an der Sperre anstehen lassen!

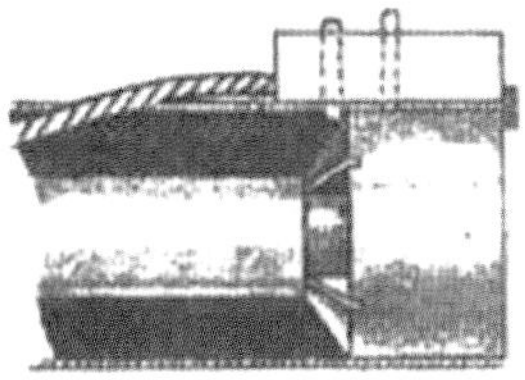

Die große **Gewehr-Panzergranate** aus dem Schießbecher verschossen, durchschlägt 80 mm Panzerung. Bis auf 100 m kannst Du damit schießen!

Die Leuchtpistole als Kampfpistole mit dem **Panzerwurfkörper 42 LP** ist ebenfalls eine sehr wirksame Waffe. Du schaffst auch damit eine 55 mm starke Panzerung. Wirkungsbereich: 30—50 m.

Merke: Alle diese Nahkampfwaffen haben fast keine Splitterwirkung, Zum Schießen auf Infanterieziele sind sie nicht erfunden! Nimm Dir lieber vor: Jede Panzerfaust ein Panzer! Suche Dir, wo's irgend geht, steile Zielflächen aus. Es gibt sonst Abrutscher!

KENNST DU DEINE WAFFEN?

An Nahkampfmitteln gibt es viele.
Nur ihre Kenntnis führt zum Ziele.

Achtung!
Graukopfzünder ohne Verzögerung!

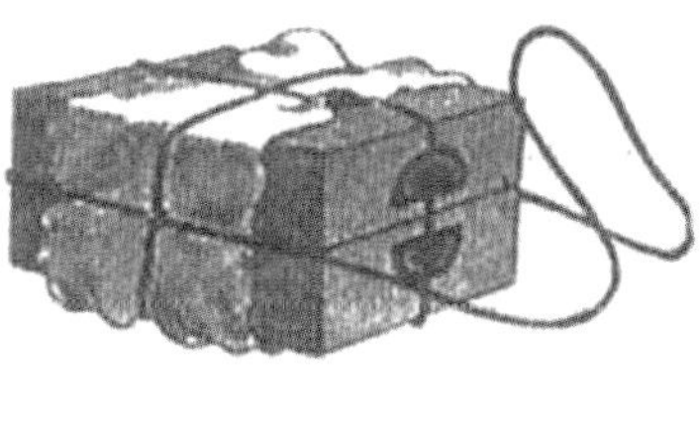

Da gibt es zunächst die **Sprengmittel:** Wenn Du noch eine **Hafthohlladung** hast, verlaß Dich auf sie! Sie ist eine hundertfach bewährte Waffe. Sie schlägt in Panzerplatten auch über 100 mm ein Loch von 3 bis 5 cm Durchmesser. Sie wirkt innen vernichtend.

Von den Waffen, die ursprünglich nicht für das Panzerknacken gedacht sind, die aber immer wieder Erfolg hatten, merke Dir vor allem die **T-Mine** und die geballte **3-Kilo-Ladung.** T-Minen und Ladungen über 5 kg durchschlagen mittlere Panzerplatten (z. B. Turmdeckel), auch wenn sie nicht eingeklemmt „verdämmt" sind. Sie heben Türme ab und haben im Innern starke Wirkung durch Schalldruck und Erschütterung.

Das wirksamste **Blendmittel** ist der **Blendkörper.** Er wirkt, sobald das Glas zerspringt. Er blendet nicht nur, sondern macht auch das Atmen im Kampfraum unmöglich. Der Qualm hält sich einige Minuten. Die **Nebelhandgranate** wirkt nach $4^1/_2$ Sekunden. Ihr Qualm hält sich ebenfalls etwa $2^1/_2$ Minuten.

Einen Panzer mit **Brandmitteln** zu zerstören, ist nicht leicht. Es verspricht Erfolg, wenn der Wagen steht. Die **Brandflaschen** enthalten eine sehr leicht brennbare Flüssigkeit. Die muß aber erst angezündet werden. Dazu gibt's Sturmstreichhölzer. Als Hilfsmittel ist die Brandflasche durchaus brauchbar.

DU MUSST DIR NUR ZU HELFEN WISSEN!

Ein Mittel an der falschen Stelle
Versagt jedoch auf alle Fälle.

Die zweite Forderung an den Panzerknacker heißt:

Im Schlaf die Waffen beherrschen. Was nützt die stärkste Waffe, wenn Du nicht verstehst, sie richtig anzuwenden!

Wenn Du die vorigen Seiten gut gelesen und Dir die Schwächen der Panzer angesehen hast, dann kannst Du Dir selber denken, wozu sich jede Waffe eignet, wo und wie Du sie anbringst. Mit einem Taschenmesser kannst Du keinen Baum fällen und mit einer Axt keinen Bleistift spitzen. Alles, wo es hingehört:

Panzerfaust, Panzerschreck, Gewehrpanzergranate und Panzerwurfkörper auf möglichst steile Flächen! Sonst kann es Abrutscher geben.

Hafthohlladungen dahin, wo auch wirklich innen etwas Wichtiges zerstört wird.

Blendkörper nur auf den Panzer selbst. Am besten auf den Bug, dann zieht der ganze Qualm in den Kampfraum.

Wenn Du keinen Blendkörper hast, bleibt Dir immer noch die Nebelhandgranate.

Zwei Pole oben!

IM SCHLAF DIE WAFFEN BEHERRSCHEN!

Es ist kein Mittel so gering,
Daß es im Notfall nicht mal ging.

Sprengmittel unter den Turmvorsprung oder auf den Motorraum! Auch Luken und Turmdeckel sind empfindlich gegen Sprengwirkung. T-Minen und geballte Ladungen mit Lappen umwickeln, mit Drahthaken versehen oder Gummiringe darüberspannen. Sonst bleiben sie nicht auf dem Panzer liegen.

Brandmittel vor allem auf das Heck! Damit das Zeug in den Motorraum läuft. Die Motorenlüftung ist dafür günstig.

Vergiß nicht die Waffe, die in der Not am wichtigsten ist: Deine Findigkeit! Ob Du nun zum Knacken ein paar Handgranaten zur geballten Ladung machst oder ob Du Sprengbüchsen nimmst, es gibt nur ein Gebot: Gebrauche, was Du hast. Anzünden kann man den Panzer im Notfall auch mit einem Benzinkanister, den man durchlöchert und mit einer drangebundenen Nebelhandgranate zündet.

Behelfsmittel gibt's viele. Regel gibt's dafür nur eine: Gebrauche, was Du hast.

DER ZWECK HEILIGT DIE MITTEL!

Selbst in der äußersten Erregung
Bewahre klare Überlegung.

So, nun kennst Du die Karten. Deine und seine. Jetzt kommt's darauf an, wer besser spielt. Er ist vor dem Kopf dicker, also mußt Du im Kopf heller sein. Männer stehen gegen Material. Deshalb:

ERST WÄGEN!

Was für ein Typ ist der, den ich knacken will?
für Schwächen hat er und
für besondere Tücken?

Also was für Waffen muß ich anwenden?
muß ich dabei überlegen?

Wie greift er an? Allein, oder sind's mehrere?
ist er unterstützt? Durch aufgesessene
oder mitlaufende Schützen?

Also wie müssen mir die Kameraden helfen?

Wo kommt er?
steht er?
ist das Gelände für ihn schwierig?
ist es für mich günstig?

Also wo bringe ich ihn zum Halten?
greife ich ihn an?
nehme ich vor der Detonation Deckung?

ERST WÄGEN, DANN WAGEN!

Was hilft des Knackers ganzes Können,
Wenn seine Kameraden pennen.

Das alles erfasse blitzschnell und

DANN WAGEN!

Die dritte Forderung ist: wie eine Fußballmannschaft zusammenarbeiten.
Im großen muß der Panzer von der begleitenden Infanterie schon getrennt sein. Aber einzelne aufgesessene oder mitlaufende Schützen könnt Ihr mit MG., MP. und Karabiner leicht vom Panzer herunterjagen und von ihm trennen, vernichten oder in Deckung zwingen, kurz, Euch vom Leibe halten. Immer:

Erst Infanterie bekämpfen - notfalls ruhig überrollen lassen.

Während Du rangehst, lenken die Sicherer die Besatzung von Dir ab. Sie nehmen ihr die Sicht und verhindern, daß sie die Luken und Nahkampföffnungen zur Abwehr öffnet. Zu diesem Zweck knallt bis zur letzten Pistole und Leuchtpistole alles, was in der Nähe ist, auf Schlitze und Optik des Panzers. Wenn eine Luke geöffnet wird, dann geben die Sicherer einen derartigen Dunst, daß sie schleunigst wieder zuklappt. Natürlich schützen Dich Deine Kameraden auch gegen Überraschungen von außen. Mußt Du ganz an den Panzer rangehen, dann ist

beim Knacken selbst diese Bedrohung von außen am größten. Dafür sind Deine Kameraden da. Die müssen aufpassen wie die Schießhunde. Kein Feind darf einen Finger rühren können. In der Verständigung mit allen Kameraden, die in der Nähe liegen, darf es jetzt keinen Zweifel geben. Sonst bist Du endlich an den Panzer ran und dann jagt Dich eine eigene Waffe wieder runter. Wenn Du Deine Sprengmittel gezündet hast, brülle laut: „Brennt!"

WIE EINE FUSSBALLMANNSCHAFT ZUSAMMENARBEITEN!

Nur mit dem Nötigsten bepackt,
Der kluge Mann den Panzer knackt.

Zum Rankommen

an den Panzer laß alles weg, was Du nicht brauchst: Gasmaske, Brotbeutel, Spaten. Vergiß aber nicht, immer eine schußbereite Pistole in der Tasche oder im Stiefelschaft zu haben.

Oft mußt Du den Gegner erst zum Langsamfahren oder zum Halten bringen. Am besten machst Du das mit Blendkörpern. Die mußt Du aber richtig auf den Kasten draufkriegen, sonst sind sie nutzlos. Das Werfen von Zwillingshandgranaten (2 Nb.Hgr. lose verbunden) über das Geschützrohr will gelernt sein. Wer im Verlegen von Minen ausgebildet ist, kann einen Panzer auch damit aufhalten. Aber die Minen unter den Panzer zu werfen oder zu schieben, das laß sein. Du verbrennst Dir dabei nur die Finger. Du kommst nämlich nicht mehr in Deckung.

Beim Anhalten überlege: Wo steht er für mich am günstigten?

Wenn Blendkörper auf dem Panzer selbst platzen, wird meist die Besatzung gleich ausbooten. Dann sofort schießen. Das Aussteigen ist der günstigste Moment. So fällt Dir der Kahn unversehrt in die Hand, und Beutepanzer sind mehr wert als Trümmerhaufen. Aber kannst Du ihn nicht sofort wegholen, dann zerstöre ihn restlos, sonst holt ihn sich der Feind.

Steht der Wagen schon, dann ist der springende Punkt die Unterstützung. Die Leute im Panzer dürfen gar nicht dazu kommen, auf Dich zu achten. Du aber nütze jeden Grasbüschel aus. Blende den Gegner, sobald es geht. Dann spring ihn an! Es geht um alles! Nur durch Schneid rettest Du Dein Leben und das Deiner Kameraden. Wenn einer weich wird, halt ihn fest. Er wird Dir nachher dafür dankbar sein.

LIEBER SCHWEISS ALS BLUT!

16

Was man von fern besorgen kann,
Dazu pirscht man sich nicht erst an.

Panzerfaust und Panzerschreck

ersparen Dir das unmittelbare Rangehen! Aber auch hier gilt: Wer wegläuft, stirbt! Volle Deckung! Jede Bewegung verrät Dich! Behalt die Nerven und laß den Panzer auf Dich zukommen! Gut getarnt ist halb geknackt, denn nicht immer hast Du ein Panzerdeckungsloch.

Tut er Dir nicht den Gefallen, auf Dich zuzufahren, dann pirsch Dich auf Schußentfernung an ihn heran.

Mit Panzerfaust und Panzerschreck mußt Du nur ruhig zielen! Der erste Schuß sitzt!

GUT GETARNT IST HALB GEKNACKT!

17

Geht es das erstemal daneben,
Dann wird's erst recht nicht aufgegeben

Mußt Du ganz an den Kerl ran, dann kommt jetzt das Schwerste:

Das Knacken

Da heißt s: Du oder er!

Keine Nahkampföffnung, keine Luke aus den Augen lassen. Denk dran: Wenn Du ihn zerstörst, dann schnell und gründlich. Bist Du erst mal in günstiger Stellung, dann pack ihm alle Sprengmittel auf, die Du hast. Nicht nervös werden. Bring das Zeug fest an und so, wie Du's gelernt hast. Abziehen nicht vergessen! Und dann schleunigst wieder in Deckung. Dicht an den Boden pressen! Hände unter den Körper! Front zur Detonation. Mund auf, Augen zu! Stahlhelmrand an die Erde! Aber sofort! Nicht erst weit weglaufen. Hast Du ihn nicht zum Halten gebracht, klappt es nicht aufs erstemal, fährt er weiter, dann nicht lockerlassen. Er muß platzen. Von hinten ran ist sogar noch günstiger.

NICHT LOCKERLASSEN, ER MUSS FALLEN!

18

Die Lage wird erst dann beschissen,
Wenn wir uns nicht zu helfen wissen.

Hast Du nichts als Deinen Schneid und ein paar Handgranaten, auch dann bist Du noch nicht verraten!

Rauf auf den Kahn!

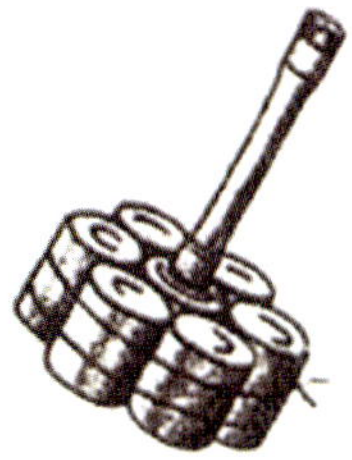

Verkauf Dein Leben so teuer als möglich! Denn erstens rettest Du Dich damit und zweitens fügst Du dem Feind empfindliche Verluste zu. Wenn einmal ein Panzer in die Luft fliegt oder zwei, dann kriegen's die anderen mit der Angst. Dem in seinem fahrbaren Sarg ist auch nicht mehr wohl. Also drauf!

Achtung! Panzerfaust und Panzerschreck machen kampfunfähig, zerstören aber nicht immer! Der Iwan schleppt die tollsten Wracks noch ab. Also sprengen! Sonst ist der Kasten in ein paar Wochen wieder auf der Bildfläche!

Lach nicht zu früh! Ist der Panzer geknackt, dann werde nicht vor Freude unvorsichtig. Achte auf feindliche Schützen und auf andere Panzer!

Laß nie zu Unvorsichtigkeiten
Dich durch Begeisterung verleiten!

BEHELFSMITTEL FORDERN GANZE KERLE!

19

Schafft Euch heran, soviel nur geht,
Wenn Panzer kommen, ist's zu spät!

Wie das auf den bisherigen Seiten steht, so ist's meistens. In der Verteidigung aber ist oft Zeit, die Panzernahbekämpfung vorzubereiten. Dazu gehört erst einmal, daß Du in Deinem Abschnitt jeden Stein und jeden Busch kennst. Verstärkt wird das Gelände durch Sperren und Gräben. Je nach der Zeit, die Ihr habt, erst Scheinsperren anlegen, dann behelfsmäßige und schließlich feste. Als Scheinsperren genügen oft Schilder „Vorsicht, Minen!" oder ein Aufkratzen der Erde, als ob Minen drunter verlegt wären.

Dadurch kriegst Du die Panzer dorthin, wo für Dich das Gelände günstig ist, und da legst Du dann Minen und gräbst Panzerdeckungslöcher.

Panzerdeckungslöcher sehen so aus:

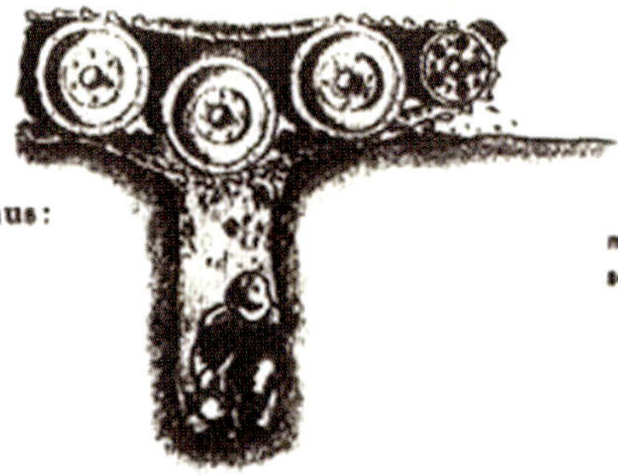

mannstief und schulterbreit

Minensperren verlegen im allgemeinen Pioniere. Ihr aber beschafft Euch rechtzeitig Nahkampfmittel. Gebt keine Ruhe, bis das Zeug herangeholt ist. Zuviel kann man davon nie haben. Die Nahkampfmittel werden auf zahlreiche trockene Depots verteilt. Die muß vom Kommandeur bis zum kleinsten Mündungsschoner jeder kennen. Wenn nichts rankommt, dann schafft Euch selbst Behelfsmittel: Brandflaschen, Benzinkanister mit Nebelhandgranaten dran, geballte Ladungen und Beutesprengmittel.

DENKT ZEITIG DRAN: SCHAFFT EUCH WAS RAN!

20

10 GEBOTE

für den Gebrauch der Panzernahkampfmittel

1. Gebot

Ob Panzerfaust, ob Panzerschreck,
Grundsätzlich heißt's: geh' hinten weg!

2. Gebot Panzerschreck

Granate fest beim Laden fassen
Und an der Sperre anstehn lassen.

3. Gebot Panzerschreck

Jedoch bedenke vor dem Laden:
Vorstecker raus aus den Granaten!

4. Gebot Gewehr-Panzergranate

Halt hoch an, sonst gibt's Kurzschuß oft
Und nicht den Treffer, den man hofft.

5. Gebot Kampfpistole

Bei Schüssen unter 30 Meter:
Kopf in den Dreck – sonst reut's Dich später.

6. Gebot Hafthohlladung

Nimm nur den Gelbkopfzünder her,
Sonst kriegst die Deckung Du nicht mehr.

7. Gebot Hafthohlladung

So angeklebt — weiß jedes Kind —
Daß 2 der Pole oben sind.

8. Gebot Blendkörper

Zart damit umgehn jedenfalls,
Sonst steigt der Qualm Dir in den Hals.

9. Gebot Brandflaschen

$^1/_3$ Flammöl, Sprit 2 Teile.
Auch andres Öl geht in der Eile.

10. Gebot Brandflaschen

Brandflaschen, wenn die Sonne sticht,
Die platzen, ob Du willst, ob nicht.

DUMMHEIT IST GEFÄHRLICH!

21

Parole heißt hier: Kampf dem Schema!
Mehr als bei jedem andren Thema.

Laßt ruhige Zeiten nicht ungenützt!

Übung ist alles! **Typ erkennen, Schwächen wissen, im Schlaf die Waffen beherrschen, wie eine Fußballmannschaft zusammenarbeiten,** das müßt Ihr können. Jeder muß es können. Nicht wie einer, der sein Leben lang nichts anderes als rechten Verteidiger gespielt hat. Das Panzerknacken muß jeder Soldat beherrschen wie seine Knarre. Ganz gleich, welche Waffe, gleich ob Grenadier oder Feldbäcker. Die Besten erst werden als Panzernahkämpfer besonders ausgebildet, wie man auch die besten Schützen als Scharfschützen hernimmt. Die trainieren sich dann zu einem **Panzernahkampftrupp** zusammen. Wenn es dafür überhaupt eine Regel gibt, dann sieht der so aus:

Ein Zerstörer, der führt den Trupp.
Ein Sicherer, der muß ein geriebener MG.-, MP.- und Karabinerschütze sein.
Ein anderer Sicherer, der außerdem Träger ist.

So kann das eingeteilt werden. Aber denkt immer daran: Kein Schema! Der Panzer fährt nicht dorthin, wo ein Panzernahkampftrupp ist. Drum noch einmal:

Jeder muß das Knacken können. Seid nicht stur! Drängt Euch dazu, das Zeug zu sehen und zu lernen! Schafft Nahkampfwaffen und Nahkampfmittel bei oder macht Euch selber welche! Und laßt sie nicht verrotten, wenn einmal eine Zeitlang nichts passiert. Vor allem Zünder, Zündladungen und Zündschnüre gut aufbewahren. Zu jeder Minute müßt Ihr auf Panzer gefaßt sein.

J E D E R Z E I T K A M P F B E R E I T !

22

23

Panzerknacker! *Konnt' einst der Panzer Dich erschüttern,*
So muß er heut vor Dir erzittern.
Du siehst, die Zeiten ändern sich,
Heut knackst Du ihn, drum kann er Dich!

Gefährlicher als der Panzer selbst ist der Schreck, den er erzeugt. Schieß ein paarmal mit den neuen Waffen, dann merkst Du: Der Panzer ist den Schreck nicht wert. Im Gegenteil, wir haben den Spieß umgedreht. Jeder, der die Waffen beherrscht, wird zum Schrecken für den Panzer. Wir stellen Männer gegen Material. Den Kampf nehmen wir auf, den Kampf Männer gegen Panzer. Wir zeigen, daß wir ihn erfolgreich führen. Und von Tag zu Tag wird er noch wirksamer, noch bedrohlicher für den Feind: Mehr Waffen, bessere Waffen und mit jedem geknackten Panzer größere Erfahrung!

STÄHLERNE HERZEN GEGEN STÄHLERNE MASSEN!

24

English Translation of Pamphlet 77/3 – Manual for the Close-Range Tank Attacker

Page 44

The Tank Cracker

Pamphlet 77/3

Manual for the Close-Range Tank Attacker

You too ...

... can crack tanks!

To do it you need guts and presence of mind. Above all else, however, superior skill triumphs!

Think about it: tanks don't just come where there are anti-tank guns. Every day tanks slip through somewhere. You, too, can suddenly find yourself facing one of these crates. Everyone, whether in the rear echelon or the most forward trench, can find himself in this situation some day. The tank won't bother to ask whether you've been trained in cracking tanks or the like.

Anybody can do it – including you!

Page 45

Army High Command
Army General Staff/The Panzer Officer

OKH Headquarters, 13 May 1944

Pamphlet 77/3

"THE TANK CRACKER"
(Manual for the Close-Range Tank Attacker)

of 13 May 1944 is to be issued to the individual soldiers to supplement their training in close-range anti-tank tactics.

A tank every 150 meters

What many others can do daily, is just as possible for you.

More than 10,000 German soldiers wear the Badge for the Singlehanded Destruction of Tanks. That many knocked-out tanks is equivalent to the equipment of 200 Russian tank brigades and the entire Russian tank output for six months.

And all this with just primitive means. They were wielded by fearless men, however, and that's what counts.

You ask yourself how that is possible under such unequal conditions? It's quite easy to explain: first of all the tank seeks out equivalent opponents: tanks, anti-tank guns and anti-aircraft guns. At the start it's not interested in you. And then watch out:

YOU TOO CAN CRACK TANKS!

Page 46

Even the most powerful tank
has certain weaknesses.

Have you ever taken part in an attack with tanks? Or have you ever ridden in a tank? If you have, you will have immediately realized that the contest of men against tanks is not quite so unequal, for

Even a tank has its weaknesses!

It sees poorly, especially what is happening directly around it.
It hears poorly.

It is ill equipped to defend against you, especially at close range.

It is strongly dependent on the terrain.

You must know the tank's weaknesses. You will find precise details for every type in the Tank Close Combat Tables (appendix to H.Dv. 469/4). Find a copy and study it! The first requirement of the tank cracker is: know the types! Know their weaknesses! And of course: observe, observe, observe!

MORE DANGEROUS THAN THE TANK ITSELF

You only stand a chance of success,
if you know its weaknesses.

His attire is worn in places.

Note the common weak spots depicted in this illustration.
This is only a schematic drawing, however.

SIDE

Gun
Gun mantlet
Vision port
Ventilator
Running gear
Turret ring

FRONT

Hatches
Optics
Weapon and mantlet
Turret ring
Machine-gun and vision port
Running gear
Final drive

REAR

Hatches
Turret ring
Hatches
Running gear

So the tank, too,
has weak spots!

There is no basic recipe for the location of these spots, so imprint them in your memory!

IS THE FEAR THAT IT CREATES!

Page 47

You must immediately recognize these most important types. Only then is there any point in memorizing their weak spots.

First notice the elegant shape
with sloped surfaces, rounded edges,
five road wheels, study them closely.
For that is the T-34.

If it has sharp edges, vertical surfaces,
six road wheels, massive shape,
is large in stature,
then it is a KV I.

The powerful KV 85 often makes
its dangerous presence felt;
chassis of the KV I,
larger turret, rounded edges, fast.

I tell you truthfully, from the front
the Sherman poses quite a threat.
It is quite fast, always look for:
six road wheels, rounded edges, maneuverable.

We can recognize the Churchill
by its many but small road wheels.
Vertical surfaces. Despite its large
tracks it is pitifully cumbersome.

Low-slung, fast vehicle
with two sets of three road wheels,
then it must be a Valentine:
fast but not very powerful.

Thoroughly study the latest tank recognition tables!
(Appendix to H.Dv. 469 2 or 2b)

Dangers are half averted, as soon as we identify them correctly!

The tank isn't entirely defenseless against close-range attack. It has defense openings through which crewmen can shoot pistols and submachine-guns and through which they can throw hand grenades. Rearward-firing machine-guns are also dangerous. All you need to know: where does it look easiest to me? Where is there danger?

Note: with hand grenades it can even reach blind spots.

WATCH OUT, THERE IS DANGER HERE!

Page 48

Weight poses no threat to you, rather it is more troublesome for him.

EVERY TANK
must halt if it is to shoot accurately. But that also makes it easier for you to approach it. Therefore: if it doesn't do it by itself, force it to stop! First examine the terrain! For every tank relies heavily on the terrain. The heavier it is, the more cumbersome also. In complex terrain its poor view becomes even poorer. You must lure it to a place that has the best cover but the best obstacles as well, and stop it there. If none is provided by nature then make one.

Such a barricade cannot of course seriously impede a tank. But it will hold it up briefly, forcing it to move slowly, lose its overall view, and that is your moment. Now you can take him out.

THE HEAVIER, THE MORE CUMBERSOME!

To be effective, one must take advantage of weak spots.

Stop!
Steady on. First you must learn several important things. A boxer who is on his toes always watched for his opponent's weak spots and hits him wherever he finds such a spot. Do exactly the same thing!

You know it looks bad. So stay still. He who runs, dies. Anyway, you can deprive it of its already limited sight. For this you have blinding devices. Also fire your hand-held weapons at vision slits and sights. Use your flare pistol too, even though it is not particularly effective. If the tank is stationary, slits are not especially difficult to hit.

The tank's poor hearing benefits your communications with your comrades. But exercise caution if the motor isn't running!

You know that it cannot effectively defend itself at close range. You are therefore safest in the blind spots close to the tank. Remember: he who runs away, dies. You must get close to the fellow, even if you have no panzerschreck, no panzerfaust. You can easily keep an eye on his few self-defense openings.

This is what the man in the tank sees.

HE WHO RUNS, DIES!

Page 49

With courage and your close-range weapons, you can take on even the most powerful tank.

Your strength is courage and determination. Your weapons are the best there are today:

First and foremost you have the Panzerfaust. It is your most important weapon. It saves you having to stalk the tank. All it demands of you is a cool head. It does everything else itself. It can penetrate 200 mm of armor and is accurate provided you aim carefully. The combat range of your panzerfaust is clearly marked on the head and sight.

The Panzerschreck is almost as simple. With it you can remain even farther away from the tank. It can penetrate 160 mm of armor and has a range of up to 150 meters.

The large Anti-Tank Rifle Grenade, fired from the rifle discharger cup, can penetrate 80 mm of armor. You can fire it from up to 100 meters.

When used as a combat pistol with the 42 LP Armor-Piercing Round, the flare pistol is also a very effective weapon. With it you can penetrate 55 mm of armor. Effective range: 30-50 m.

Note: Almost all of these close-range weapons have almost no fragmentation effect. They were not conceived for use against infantry targets! Rule of thumb: one tank for every panzerfaust! When necessary, seek targets with vertical surfaces in order to avoid ricochets!

DO YOU KNOW YOUR WEAPON?

There are many types of close-range weapon,knowledge of them is necessary for success.

First there are Explosive Devices: If you have a Hollow Charge Magnetic Mine, rely on it! It is a weapon that has proved itself hundreds of times over. It creates a 3- to 5-cm diameter hole even in armor plate more than 100 mm thick. Its effect on the interior is devastating.

Of the weapons not originally conceived for use against tanks, the most important are the T-Mine and the concentrated 3-Kilo Charge. T-mines and charges over 5 kg can penetrate medium armor plate (e.g. turret roofs), even if they are not fixed in place. They can dislodge turrets and cause severe internal damage through acoustic pressure and concussion.

The most effective Blinding Device is the Smoke Charge. It begins working as soon as the glass is broken. It not only blinds, but also makes breathing impossible in the fighting compartment. The smoke lasts for several minutes. The Smoke Hand Grenade is effective after 4½ seconds. Its smoke lasts approximately 2½ minutes.

Destroying a tank with a Flame Device is not easy. It is most effective when the tank is stopped. Fire Bottles contain a flammable liquid, however they must be lit before use. For this there are assault matches. As a makeshift weapon the flame bottle is entirely practical.

YOU ONLY HAVE TO KNOW HOW TO HELP YOURSELF!

Page 50

Placing a weapon in the wrong place will always result in failure.

The second requirement of the tank cracker is:
Mastery of your weapons. What good is the most powerful weapon if you don't understand how to use it properly!

If you have read the previous pages well and have examined the weaknesses of the various tanks, then you can decide for yourself what each weapon is best suited for and where and how to employ it. You can't cut down a tree with a pocket knife or sharpen a pencil with an axe. Everything where it belongs:

Whenever possible, use the panzerfaust, panzerschreck, anti-tank rifle grenade and armor-piercing flare pistol round against near-vertical surfaces! Otherwise ricochets can result.
Hollow charge magnetic mines where there is something really important inside to destroy.
Blinding devices only on the tank itself. The best place is the front, then smoke will enter the fighting compartment.
If you do not have a blinding device, you still always have smoke grenades.

MASTER YOUR WEAPONS!

There is no weapon so small, that it cannot be used in an emergency.

Explosives under the turret overhang or on the engine compartment! Hatches and the turret roof are also vulnerable to explosive effect. Wrap T-mines and concentrated charges with cloth, attach wire hooks, or stretch rubber bands over them. Otherwise they will not remain on the tank.

Whenever possible, flame weapons on the rear decking. In this way the contents can run into the engine compartment. The engine ventilator is ideally suited for this.

Don't overlook the weapon that is the most important in an emergency: your resourcefulness! Whether you use a few hand grenades to make a concentrated charge or employ demolition blocks to knock out a tank, there is just one rule: use what you have. In an emergency you can even set a tank on fire with a gasoline can, punching a hole in it and igniting it with a smoke grenade tied to the can.

There are many makeshift solutions, but there is only one rule for their use: use what you have.

THE END JUSTIFIES THE MEANS!

Page 51

Keep a clear head, even in the most stressful situations!

So, now you know the cards. Yours and his. What matters now is who plays better. He head is thicker, therefore your head must be clearer. It is man against materiel.

FIRST WEIGH THE SITUATION!

WHAT type is it that I want to knock out!
weaknesses does he have and what special tricks?
Therefore what kind of weapon should I use?
must I take into consideration?
HOW is he attacking? Alone, or are there several?
is he supported? By riding or walking riflemen?
Therefore how must my comrades assist me?
WHERE is he coming?
is he positioned?
is the terrain difficult for him?
is it favorable for me?
Therefore where can I force him to halt?
should I attack him?
take cover from the explosion?

WEIGHT THE SITUATION FIRST, THEN ACT!

What good are all the cracker's skills, if his comrades are asleep!

Grasp everything quickly and

THEN ACT!

The third requirement is: work together like a football team.
As a general rule the tank must already be separated from its escorting infantry. But you can easily use your machine-gun, submachine-gun or carbine to chase single walking or riding riflemen away from the tank and separate them from it, destroy them or force them to take cover, in short, keep them at bay. Always: Engage the infantry first – if necessary remain still and allow them to pass by. While you approach, your supporting troops will distract the crew, depriving it of its sight and preventing it from opening hatches and self-defense ports. For this purpose, to the end pistols and flare pistols are fired at the tank's vision slits and sight apertures. If a hatch is opened, the support troops lay down such heavy fire as to cause it to be closed immediately. Of course you also protect your comrades against external surprises. If you must go right up to the tank, then this threat from outside is greatest while knocking out the tank. That is why your comrades are there. They must watch like hawks. No enemy must be able to move a finger. There can be no uncertainty in communications with nearby comrades, otherwise you may be cut down by one of your own men when you finally reach the tank. When you have lit the fuse of your explosive device, loudly shout: "It's lit!"

WORK TOGETHER LIKE A FOOTBALL TEAM!

Page 52

The wise man only takes what he needs to knock out the tank.

Before approaching

the tank, leave behind everything you do not need: gas mask, rations bag, entrenching tool. But don't forget to always have a loaded pistol in your pocket of shaft of your boot.

Often you must first force the enemy to slow down or stop. This is best achieved with blinding devices. You must correctly place them on the tank however, otherwise they are useless. The tossing of twin hand grenades (2 smoke grenades tied loosely together) over the barrel of the gun should be learned. Those trained in the use of mines can also use them to stop a tank. But don't try tossing or pushing the mines under the tank. You'll only burn your fingers, meaning you'll never reach cover.

Before stopping [the tank], consider: what place is most favorable for me?

If blinding devices explode on the tank itself, the crew will usually abandon their vehicle at once. That is the most favorable moment. The beast falls into your hands intact, and captured tanks are more valuable than piles of wreckage. But if you can't remove it immediately, destroy it completely, otherwise the enemy will recover it.

If the tank is already stopped, then the crucial point is your support. The people inside the tank must never be given a chance to turn their attention to you. But you exploit every tuft of grass. Blind the enemy as soon as possible. Then attack! It's all or nothing! Only through boldness can you save your life and those of your comrades. If someone begins to waver, hold him fast. He will thank you for it later.

BETTER SWEAT THAN BLOOD!

What one can accomplish from a distance, alleviates the need to close in first.

Panzerfaust and Panzerschreck

spare you from going right up to the tank! But here too the rule applies: he who runs away, dies! Stay in cover! Any movement can betray your position! Keep your nerves and let the tank come to you! Good camouflage is half the job, for you will not always have a foxhole.

If he doesn't do you the courtesy of heading towards you, then stalk him until you are in firing range.

With the panzerfaust and panzerschreck you must aim carefully! The first round will be on target!

Caution! Flame jet!

GOOD CAMOUFLAGE IS HALF THE JOB!

Page 53

Don't give up, if the first shot misses.

If you must go right up to the tank, then comes the hardest part:

Knocking it out

That means: you or he!

Don't take your eyes off any self-defense port, any hatch. Remember: if you intend to destroy him, do it quickly and thoroughly. Once you have reached a favorable position, then place all the explosives on it that you have. Don't become nervous. Place the charge securely, the way you were taught. Don't forget to activate the fuse. And then take cover as quickly as possible. Hug the ground! Hands beneath your body! Face the detonation. Mouth open, eyes closed! Rim of your steel helmet on the ground! But immediately! Don't try to run away first. If you fail to stop him, if your first attempt fails, if he keeps moving, don't give up. He must be destroyed. Approaching from the rear is even better.

DON'T GIVE UP, HE MUST FALL!

The situation only becomes shitty, when we don't know how to help ourselves.

You still have a chance, even if all you have is your courage and a few hand grenades.

Get up on the boat!

Make them pay the highest price possible for your life! By doing so you will save yourself and inflict heavy losses on the enemy. If you blow up one or two tanks you will strike fear into the others. The men in the mobile coffins will lose confidence. So after them!

Caution! Panzerfaust and panzerschreck disable but don't always destroy! The Ivan even recovers badly-wrecked tanks. So blow them up! Otherwise the crates will be back in the picture in a few weeks!

Don't laugh too soon! Don't allow your joy over destroying the tank make you careless. Watch for enemy soldiers and other tanks!

Don't let your enthusiasm cause you to become careless!

IT TAKES A REAL MAN TO USE IMPROVIZED WEAPONS!

Page 54

Make every possible preparation, when the tanks come it's too late!

The descriptions on the previous pages depict how it usually is, but in the defense there is often time to make preparations to engage tanks from close range. The first thing is to know every stone and every bush in your sector. Enhance the natural terrain with obstacles and ditches. Depending on the amount of time you have, first set up mock barricades, then makeshift and finally permanent ones. Often, a few "Caution, Mines!" signs or scratches in the surface of the earth, suggesting the placement of mines, provide adequate mock barricades.

In this way you get the tanks to go to where the terrain favors you, and then you lay mines and dig tank defense holes there.

Tank defense holes look like this: man-deep and shoulder-wide.

As a rule pioneers lay the mines, but obtain close-range anti-tank weapons from them on a timely basis. Do not rest until the weapons have been delivered. One can never have too many of them. Close-range anti-tank weapons are held in numerous dry depots. Everyone must know where they are, from the commanding officer to the most junior soldier. If nothing comes, then procure makeshift weapons for yourself: flame bottles, gasoline cans with attached smoke grenades, concentrated charges and captured explosives.

REMEMBER: PROCURE WHAT YOU NEED!

10 RULES
for the use of close-range anti tank weapons

1st Rule
Whether panzerfaust or panzerschreck,
the basic rule is: stay away from the back end!

2nd Rule Panzerschreck
Grip the projectile firmly when loading,
and line it up against the stop.

3rd Rule Panzerschreck
Before loading, however, remember:
remove the pins from the rounds!

4th Rule Anti-Tank Rifle Grenade
Aim high, otherwise there will often be
short shots, and not the hit you hoped for.

5th Rule Flare Pistol
When shooting from less than 30 meters:
head in the mud—or you'll regret it later.

6th Rule Hollow Charge Magnetic Mine
Take only the yellow fuses,
or else you'll never make it to cover.

7th Rule Hollow Charge Magnetic Mine
As any child knows, stick it so
that two of the feet are facing up.

8th Rule Blinding Devices
Always handle them gently, or else you'll
be up to your own neck in smoke.

9th Rule Fire Bottles
1/3 fuel oil, two parts gasoline.
Other types of oil will do in a pinch.

10th Rule Fire Bottles
When exposed to the sun, fire bottles will
explode whether you want them to or not.

STUPIDITY IS DANGEROUS!

Page 55

The motto here is: fight according to the scheme! More than in any other situation.

Do not allow quiet times to go unused!

Practice is everything! You must be able to identify types, master your weapons, work together like a football team. Everyone must be able to. Not like one who for a long time has done nothing but act as a proper defender. Every soldier must master tank cracking the way he does his gun. It makes no difference what weapon he wields, whether he is a grenadier or a baker. The best are given special training as tank killers, just as the best riflemen are trained as snipers. They then train themselves to become a close-range anti-tank team. If there is one rule for this, it is as follows:

A destroyer, who leads the team.
A defender, who must be a skilled shot with the machine-gun, submachine-gun and carbine.
Another defender, who is also a bearer.

All must be able to take out a tank. Don't be stubborn! Force yourselves to see the thing and learn it! Get close-range weapons and materials or make them for yourself! And don't allow them to fall into disrepair if nothing happens for a long time. Fuses, fuse charges and fuse cord in particular must be stored properly. They might have to be placed on a tank at any moment.

ALWAYS BE READY TO FIGHT!

This is what happens!

...when real men come up against masses of materiel. Recognition of this is the Special Badge for the Singlehanded Destruction of Tanks and, when possible, fourteen days leave.
Even more important though, is the realization: you have accomplished something of which you can be proud and in so doing have placed yourselves in the ranks of the bravest.

If you've roughed up a tank, you'll probably be heading off on leave soon.

Page 56

Tank Cracker: While once the tank was able to strike fear in you, now before you he trembles. You see, the times are changing. Now you take him out, instead of he you!

More dangerous than the tank itself is the fear it creates. Fire the new weapons a few times and you will realize: there is no need to fear the tank. On the contrary, we have turned the tables. Everyone who can master these weapons becomes the tank's worst nightmare! We send men against materiel. We accept battle, man against tank. We show that we can wage it successfully. And, day by day, we become more effective, more dangerous to the enemy: more weapons, better weapons and with each knocked-out tank greater experience!

HEARTS OF STEEL AGAINST STEEL MONSTERS!

Sources

Army Ordnance Gazette 1942, Part B, 14th Issue, Printing 5, p. 117, subparagraph 190
Army Ordnance Gazette 1942, Part B, 49th Issue, Printing 17, p. 409, subparagraph 688
General Army Memoranda 1943, 4th Issue, p. 79, subparagraph 119
Air Force Ordnance Gazette 1942, 35th Issue, p. 1180, subparagraph 2166
Air Force Ordnance Gazette 1944, 33rd Issue, p. 543, subparagraph 1036
Army Service Manual 469/4 dated 7 October 1943
Pamphlet 77/3 dated 13 May 1944
Doehle, Dr. Heinrich von: Die Auszeichnungen des Großdeutschen Reichs, Norderstedt 2000.
Lüdeke, Alexander: Waffentechnik im Zweiten Weltkrieg, no location, no date.
Michaelis, Rolf: Die Sturmabzeichen des Heeres, Berlin 1998.
Pawlas, Karl: Datenblätter für Heereswaffen etc., Nuremberg 1976.